WHAT ARE THE ODDS?

Blowing the Whistle on California's Lottery

Gary Reid Galbreath

What Are the Odds?

Blowing the Whistle on California's Lottery

DEFIANCE PRESS
& PUBLISHING

ISBN-13: 978-1-955937-95-5
ISBN-13: 978-1-955937-96-2

Published by Defiance Press and Publishing, LLC

Bulk orders of this book may be obtained by contacting Defiance Press and Publishing, LLC.

www.defiancepress.com

Defiance Press & Publishing, LLC
281-581-9300

info@defiancepress.com

Contents

This is a story about my time as an investigator with the California State Lottery. I worked for the lottery as a sworn investigator for the lottery's Security/Law Enforcement Division (SLED) for a little over three and a half years. I investigated hundreds of cases, which involved fraud, theft, forgery, and questionable claims during my time with the lottery. Many of these crimes could have been prevented had proper safeguards been put in place.

The most important investigation of my career was the one I launched into the lottery itself. The investigation revealed unethical conduct on the part of the executive staff appointed by the governor to oversee the operation of the lottery and the management who reported to them. Oftentimes, individuals in lottery management were hired through nepotism, which contributed to a culture of looking the other way when something wasn't right. The culture was more like a private company, as opposed to a government-run entity. The most egregious offense on the part of these individuals was the misappropriation of millions of dollars in public funds, which should have legally gone to the public education system, and the retaliation against those, including myself, who spoke out against it.

The cases and incidents discussed in this book are all true. Some dates are approximate, while others are specific. Some names have been omitted to protect the identity of victims. The facts are supported by documentation, reports, news stories, personal accounts, and legal statutes. These will be cited where appropriate. I started writing this book while I was suspended by the lottery for my whistleblowing activities, so my emotions and thought process are spread out over five years, presented in real-time. I use my opinion sparingly and stick to the facts.

State-run lotteries are a multibillion-dollar industry. In my experience, these agencies place their image above integrity. Government-operated lotteries sell their integrity and the dreams of striking it rich. When the news discusses the lottery, it's usually the frenzy around a large jackpot or an amazing story about someone's big win. People are encouraged to buy tickets using buzz words like *imagine*, *win*, and *possibilities*, all the while asking "What if?" News stories that make people question the integrity of government-run lotteries, or even worse, expose lottery retail owners and employees cheating the system, quickly disappear in favor of discussing the next big jackpot.

One example was the story of Eddie Tipton, who was employed by the Multi-State Lottery Association (MUSL) as the Information Security Director. MUSL is owned and operated by member lotteries from various states. Tipton was hired by MUSL to design the software that produced randomly selected numbers for draw games in multiple states. Tipton was a questionable choice for this position because he had prior criminal convictions for burglary and theft. Most State lotteries have a regulation that prohibits someone with a theft conviction from employment, but MUSL did not. Tipton planted an algorithm that manipulated the outcome of lottery games in five different states for almost a decade. As a result, Tipton and his accomplices received $24 million in prize money. In Tipton's confession, he said he had gone to several MUSL officials after manipulating a lottery game in Colorado. He warned them about major flaws in their operational security, but they ignored him. Tipton was eventually convicted and sentenced to up to twenty-five years in prison. Tipton claims the major flaws still haven't been addressed. (Clayworth, 2018)

The story of Tipton didn't get the media attention one would expect, which is surprising when you consider over thirty state lotteries are members of MUSL. California has even cited guidelines produced by MUSL when changing regulations for interstate games such as Powerball.

The experiences I will share do not cast a positive light on the operation of California's lottery. They call into question the honesty, integrity, and fairness of government-run lotteries across the country. When I was sworn in as a California peace officer by Paula LaBrie, the acting deputy director of California's lottery, I took my oath seriously. The oath I took was:

"I, Gary Reid Galbreath, do solemnly swear (or affirm) that I will support and defend the Constitution of the United States and the Constitution of the State of California against all enemies, foreign and domestic; that I will bear true faith and allegiance to the Constitution of the United States and the Constitution of the State of California; that I take this obligation freely, without any mental reservation or purpose of evasion; and that I will well and faithfully discharge the duties upon which I am about to enter."

I took my role as a sworn investigator seriously and believed in the mission of SLED. I was initially honored to be a part of an entity that ensured supplemental funding for public education. I was a theatre kid in high school. I came from a family of educators and public servants. I knew how important educational funding was, especially for supplemental programs. As an investigator for SLED, I was tasked with ensuring the honesty, integrity, and fairness of the operation of

California's lottery. This was the mission statement of SLED and had been since it was formed, although you can't find any mention of SLED's mission statement on the lottery's website. While the games themselves are administered in a fair and ethical manner, it's the manner in which the lottery itself is operated after the winning ticket is claimed that is deeply concerning.

I truly enjoyed most of my time as a lottery investigator. I worked some amazing cases with some amazing people. It was one of the only law enforcement jobs where most of the people you interacted with were happy to see you. Talking with individuals whose lives were changed forever after winning a large prize was always one of the best parts of the job. While my belief in the system has certainly been destroyed, I still take pride in what I did while I was there.

CHAPTER 1

The History of California's Lottery/SLED

A government-run lottery in California was presented to California voters in the form of a proposition. The proposition was sold to voters as a way to provide additional money to public schools without having to raise taxes. Proposition 37 also prohibited legal gambling in the form of casinos, ensuring a monopoly for the state lottery if the proposition were to pass. The largest finical backer of the proposition was Scientific Games, which stood to benefit financially since they were one of the only companies that could provide "secure" lottery games. The first three contracts with the lottery made Scientific Games $61.7 million. (Crabbe, 1986)

On November 6, 1984, Proposition 37 was passed by 57.9% of voters. This created the California State Lottery Act of 1984 which authorized the creation of a state government-operated lottery. A California-operated lottery was opposed by then-Governor Deukmejian, police officers, the state schools Superintendent William Honig, and many educators. Deukmejian took his time with appointing individuals to key leadership roles. (Ferrell, 1989)

The California State Lottery Act provided specific rules and regulations on how the lottery would be operated. The Lottery Act was incorporated into California's government code with some of the sections being criminally enforceable. The Lottery Act outlined requirements for who could be appointed to serve on the Lottery Commission. One of the members was required to have a background in law enforcement.

The Lottery Act required California's lottery to establish strict rules and regulations that would govern the operation of lottery games, the method for claiming prizes, and who was eligible to receive a cash prize. These regulations were intended to be the official rules of the game. California's lottery regulations govern the day-to-day operations of California's lottery. It permits lottery retail locations to pay prizes less than $600 and requires a winner to claim anything $600 or more with the lottery. These rules and regulations dictate how the lottery disperses billions of dollars to winners, lottery retail owners, contractors, vendors, and employees. (Information, 1984)

One of the specific sections of the California Lottery Act is § 8880.4, which covers allocations of revenue and maximization of funding to public education. This section specifically outlines how the surplus money generated for public schools is allocated and what happens to unclaimed prize money. This section requires that California's lottery return 87% "of the total annual revenues from the sale of state lottery tickets or shares shall be returned to the public in the form of prizes and net revenues to benefit public education." Of particular note is the word "return" because it clearly defines California lottery funds as belonging to the public.

The Lottery Act also required the appointment of a deputy director for SLED—one who was tasked with hiring a team of lottery agents, later called investigators, who would be responsible for the enforcement of laws and lottery regulations. There were multiple crimes committed during the first several years of the lottery's existence. Most of the crimes involved individuals altering losing tickets to make them look like winners in an effort to claim large sums of money. When lottery agents made arrests, there were press releases, magazine articles, and news coverage to display the integrity of California's lottery.

An article from the San Francisco Chronicle titled "Wired Tight" ran on March 5, 1989. The article featured an interview with Lew Ritter, who was the first Chief for SLED. Ritter discussed 325 people who were arrested in the first four years the lottery was in operation. He bragged about the elaborate security system put in place to protect the lottery because it was widely criticized. The article mentioned that the lottery's own research showed the heaviest gamblers who purchased lottery products came from the poorest ethnic groups. It also cited a study from UC-Riverside, which found that a "surprising" number of minors played the lottery. This article was similar to most articles discussing California's lottery in the first decade it was in operation. (Ferrell, 1989)

The executives of California's lottery were also called upon to answer to the State Assembly during the first few years it was in operation. The lottery was tasked with answering tough questions about how they were spending the public's money. This included discussing the screening process for lottery retail owners and how the lottery was being advertised. Answering to the State Assembly provided some level of accountability to the people of California. This type of accountability ultimately vanished and was replaced with Lottery Commission meetings, which occur every few months and are overseen by individuals who serve on a part-time basis.

The Lottery Commission rarely challenges lottery executives who go before them with proposals for spending millions of dollars, changing lottery regulations, and joining interstate games. The reason for the lack of oversight is the individuals who are appointed to Lottery Commission posts normally use the position as a stepping stone into politics. Most of the individuals have full-time jobs, which require the majority of their time and attention. The commissioners receive a stipend during their meetings, which pales in comparison to the salaries they receive from their full-time jobs. During my time with the lottery, the Commissioners held positions such as sheriff of Alameda County, senior vice president with the National Broadcasting Company, and principal attorney. A search of the website *Transparent California* shows that the average salary of each of the commissioners was $1,200 in 2014, and these are the individuals who approve the way billions of dollars of public money are being spent.

The lack of oversight has led to California's lottery being treated like a private business operating under the guise of being a state government agency. There is a complete lack of accountability, oversight, and a loss of integrity no one should expect from a government agency. All one has to do is look to the countless news stories over the years regarding the top personnel in the lottery—nepotism, misappropriation of public funds, drinking on the job, inappropriate behavior at publicly funded events, and retaliation against anyone who had the courage to speak up.

The internal checks and balances for California's lottery were supposed to be SLED, which was the intention of the legislation when they wrote the Lottery Act. SLED is responsible for ensuring the integrity of lottery games. This includes overseeing the production of scratch-off tickets and establishing safeguards for draw games such as Super Lotto, Powerball, and Mega Millions. SLED also established "validation" procedures for winning tickets, which are methods of confirming that tickets are legitimate. These validation methods are mostly inadequate due to the refusal of California's lottery to ensure lottery retailers are fulfilling minimum internal safeguards, which could be used to assist with investigations. This was a critical component to several cases during my time as an investigator.

One of the many interesting things I learned during my time with the lottery is that SLED would only investigate "questionable claims" and those for prizes of $350,000 or more. This meant that any claim which appeared to be routine, and any amount under $350,000 were simply paid. This led to rampant fraud from those who learned how to manipulate the system. For example, the lottery uses an internal database that tracks all incoming claims submitted by customers throughout the state. Lottery customers were, and possibly still are, required to submit claims for any prizes of $600 or more. The customers are required to complete a winner claim form, which involves answering questions related to the individual's status as a lottery retailer and whether they are a relative of a lottery retailer or an employee of a lottery retailer. Customers completing the forms are also required to sign under penalty of perjury that the information they are submitting is true and correct.

One of the many flaws in the way California's lottery handles winner claim forms as of 2016, is that they do not require a search of the database using names, social security numbers, or addresses prior to entering a new claim into the system. The system did not auto-populate or flag previous claims or claimants. This resulted in individuals claiming a prize having multiple "player identification numbers" and individuals who shared addresses with lottery retail owners not being forwarded for investigation unless another issue caught someone's attention such as Wite-Out on the form or ticket. During my time as an investigator, I had several cases that involved employees, lottery retail owners, and relatives of lottery retail owners. In most cases, they received hundreds of thousands of dollars from the state before finally being referred to SLED for an investigation.

Over the years SLED has busted up counterfeit rings, identified employees who tried to manipulate the outcomes of games, and identified trends involving dishonest lottery retail owners. In 2008 a former deputy director of SLED conducted an audit of lottery winners to identify patterns. This audit revealed a large quantity of winning tickets worth $600 or more were being claimed by retail owners, their family members, and associates. The numbers showed that the majority of winning tickets were being claimed by individuals who fell into this category, not regular players.

SLED formed a team that strategized on a way to keep retailers honest through enforcement. The team came up with an idea that would set California apart from all other lotteries by setting a standard. Decoy lottery tickets were created that looked the same as regular lottery tickets. The decoy tickets would have a value of at least $600. When the tickets were scanned at lottery terminals by a clerk, a notification popped up informing them the ticket was a winner. Per lottery regulations, the clerk would have to inform the customer they had won a prize and would need to file a claim with the lottery.

If the clerk told the customer the ticket wasn't a winner and stole it, they would have to file a claim with the lottery in order to claim the prize. When the thief filled out a claim form in order to claim the prize, they would have to sign under penalty of perjury stating they were the rightful owner of the ticket they were claiming. This only added to several felonies the suspect would face once they were arrested. The thought process was that an increased compliance rate, through enforcement, would protect lottery players.

This operation was referred to as the Retailer Compliance Program. Lottery retailers were warned that these operations would occur statewide. The Retailer Compliance Program was featured on *Dateline NBC*. An undercover investigator entered lottery retail locations posing as a customer. The Investigator presented the ticket to the clerk and asked them to check and see if the ticket was a winner. If the clerk stole the ticket and claimed it at a later date, the *Dateline NBC* reporter would return to the location with the investigator to confront the suspect and arrest them. *Dateline NBC* conducted several of these operations with lottery investigators. Similar operations were conducted by lotteries in other states. The *Dateline* specials on these operations were one of the main reasons I wanted to work for the lottery.

SLED was also tasked with assisting outside law enforcement agencies with investigations involving lottery tickets. All lottery tickets are individually numbered, which allows for tracking to see where a ticket was sold and where the ticket was checked to see if it was a winner. This comes in handy with robbery and burglary investigations because a suspect will normally wear a mask while stealing tickets. When the suspect goes to another store to cash in their winning tickets, they remove the mask. Surveillance photos of suspects cashing in stolen tickets have led to countless arrests and convictions.

SLED has always been staffed by sworn peace officers and civilians from various backgrounds. This has made SLED a top-notch organization that was once a place where many wanted to work. SLED is not well-liked within the lottery because of the work it does and the fraud it exposes. Some view SLED as being counterproductive to a sales organization, which ultimately led to a lack of enforcement and low morale, but we'll get to that later.

Lew Ritter wrote a final letter when he left SLED. The letter told the story of him being hired, and other "war stories" from his time as chief. The letter discussed his first meeting with the president of Scientific Games, who offered to purchase Ritter's dinner. Ritter refused and told him he couldn't accept anything for free from a contractor. He also discussed convincing the public that the lottery was honest and fair—and his frustrations with such matters as the way the Board of Education allocated money received from the lottery. This included citing a case in Southern California where $300,000 was spent on a Christmas party. Ritter retired on 12/31/1991. (Ritter, 1991)

CHAPTER 2

The History of Me (Abridged)

My apologies for the technical jargon in the first chapter, but I am assuming you want to understand why you're reading this book. And let me assure you in advance that I'm not a tech-savvy guy. I'm just a fast learner and a hard worker, which is why I can still rattle off some of the technical terms several years later. I can also still recite my employee identification number from my time with Blockbuster Video. Hopefully, this chapter will be a little more interesting because it's completely self-serving. I get to tell my background story.

I was born in Stockton, CA, and spent the majority of my life in Sacramento, CA. I was the product of two parents with substance-abuse issues, with one being slightly more well-rounded than the other, at least on paper. I was raised by my mother and was lucky enough to have several role models in my life who offered stability I may not have otherwise known. As a child, I was diagnosed with acute sinus problems, allergies, asthma, and a weakened immune system. This resulted in several close calls and hospital stays because everything would act up at once, leaving me unable to breathe. I remember trips to the hospital which involved being in an oxygen tent, countless surgeries, and treatments involving needles. I think facing death at a young age made me mature, to some extent, rather quickly. It also made me appreciate life and take every opportunity I could to act like a kid.

One of the first things I remember taking a serious liking to was *Ghostbusters*. I loved the movies and the cartoon. I had the toys and my own jumpsuit, which I would wear to doctor's appointments all the time and ask them to refer to me as "Dr. Venkman." The concept of *Ghostbusters* was probably a precursor to my future since it revolved around a team of paranormal investigators with a sense of humor. A large part of my youth was spent reading comic books, watching wrestling, binge-watching syndicated television shows, playing video games, and going to the movies. I truly loved all things nerd, and I still do.

My family is primarily made up of teachers, police officers, soldiers, and government employees. Needless to say, I was pretty much destined to work in some sort of public service. I spent many late nights as a child with my mom and sisters watching them grade papers. This gave me a strong respect for how hard educators work. Most teachers are grossly underpaid and spend a lot of their own time and money to make things work.

I grew up fairly poor because my mother didn't work and my father didn't pay child support. We were on public assistance, including food stamps, and spent many hours in line at local food banks on a weekly basis. Leftovers were often our only option for several consecutive days, and trips to fast-food restaurants were a gourmet experience. I learned about used needles, used condoms, violence, and gangs at a very early age. One of the men my mother dated, Mike, lived across the street from us. Mike's back porch faced an hourly motel which had fairly large windows. On occasion, we would simply enjoy the show when there were police raids or someone being hung outside of their window by their feet for whatever reason causes someone to get hung outside of a window. My early childhood was entertaining, to say the least. Mike was one of the best human beings I ever knew, and he instilled a lot of my better qualities.

In high school, I decided I wanted to be an actor. I was a fat kid who thought I could be the next Chris Farley because I loved making people laugh, even when it was at my own expense. I was a class clown who didn't take school seriously. One of my claims to fame in high school was taking sandwich fixings and making a gigantic hoagie on top of my algebra final. It seemed like a good idea considering I was terrible at math and was probably going to fail the final anyway. Despite this, I somehow managed to get a "D" in the class.

I eventually got into the drama program and auditioned for my first part in a school play. I read for the part of Oscar Unger in *The Odd Couple*. I knew I had the attention of the director when I made him laugh while reading my line. I was eventually cast as Murray, the cop, which in retrospect, is kind of ironic. I walked away with my fair share of injuries and scars from shows even though the drama program was absolutely not high school football. I had to take a big bite of a peanut butter sandwich during one scene, which took place during a poker game. The bite I took was way too big considering there was nothing for me to drink to wash it down. I sat at the poker table in a panic knowing my line was coming up. The house was packed, so I was going to look like the fat guy choking on his sandwich. I swallowed a gigantic glob of breaded peanut butter and spit out the line while almost choking to death.

I was then cast as the butler in *The Man Who Came to Dinner*. My role mostly consisted of bringing food to the other cast members and standing behind a swivel door waiting for my cue to go open the door. During another packed show, I was standing behind the swivel door with my arms resting at my side, waiting for the doorbell to ring, which was my cue. One of the cast members walked onto the stage and began acting out their scene without her prop photo album. She improvised by telling the other cast member she would be right back. She came running through the swivel door which smacked me in the face. My nose started to gush blood out of both nostrils with my cue quickly approaching. I ran to the bathroom, shoved toilet paper up my nostrils, and made it back in time for my cue like a champ. This was the closest I came in high school to playing a contact sport.

Drama taught me a lot about being comfortable with who you are. It was extremely inclusive with representatives from all walks of life interacting with one another. Gay, straight, rich, poor, and diverse backgrounds all working together. Drama also laid a foundation for my lack of nervousness in court and when speaking to large groups of people. I always felt like I was back in a play when I was on the stand in a courtroom, which really pissed off a lot of defense attorneys because they couldn't break me.

I somehow managed to graduate from high school and enrolled in some business classes in college, which weren't for me. I began searching for my calling because I realized being an actor probably wasn't going to pay the bills. One of my first decent-paying jobs, $9.25 an hour, was working as a community service guide with the Downtown Sacramento Partnership. Guides worked with law enforcement on a daily basis, which led to me looking into being a cop as a means to pay the bills. My first real law enforcement job was working as a parking enforcement officer for the local community college police department. Writing parking tickets and taking reports for stolen pencil holders seemed like a calling. At the time, I thought it was the greatest job ever and began exploring my options. I had been mostly supporting myself since I was seventeen, and the prospect of a steady income and job security was very appealing.

I spent the majority of my career working in campus law enforcement and worked as many as three jobs at a time. The jobs provided me with many interesting war stories and a strong foundation for my investigative skills. I always listened to the seasoned guys when they gave me advice. They came from a variety of backgrounds and provided me with their thoughts on what direction I should go. One of these seasoned vets told me about state investigators. I was shocked to learn how many different bureaus and regulatory agencies had enforcement units.

When I found out that lottery cops were a thing, I was sold. How awesome would it be to be a lottery investigator? My job would be protecting money that provides funding for public education. The cases would be unique and entertaining. Nobody would truly know what I did because the majority of the public had no idea you even existed. I knew this was where I wanted to work and would stay there forever if I was lucky enough to get hired. The first step was getting through a law enforcement academy because the lottery wasn't known for hiring someone who hadn't graduated from an academy.

My first job as an officer with peace officer powers was working as a public safety officer with the McGeorge School of Law. This position was as close to the major leagues as I could get without going through a full law enforcement academy. There are actually several different jobs in the state of California that provide you with peace officer powers while not working as a police officer. Some of these include gravediggers, correctional officers, and private university security. I had no idea how I got lucky enough to score the job, but I was happy to be there. I got into fights, foot pursuits, made arrests, and got to engage in community-oriented policing. It was very close to what I wanted to do, but I wasn't quite there yet.

In January of 2009, I got the call I had been waiting for. I was hired by the California Highway Patrol (CHP) as a cadet and would get paid while going through the academy. While my heart wasn't set on being AAA with a badge, the CHP offered me the opportunity to fulfill one of my dreams, which was working bike patrol in the state capital. I quit my job, gave up my health insurance, and arrived at the CHP academy on a morning so cold everyone could see their breath.

My first day was a blur of getting screamed at with over two hundred cadets and running around with no real direction because failure was part of the training. By the end of my second week, I had caught a viral infection from one of the cadets who came to the academy sick. My health insurance hadn't kicked in yet, so I went to urgent care and got Amoxicillin, which has stinky gas as a bonus side effect.

CHP physical fitness is the reason why most CHP officers are complete assholes. During Physical Training (PT), the PT staff bring in multiple CHP personnel to storm a classroom full of unsuspecting cadets. The ordeal is similar to fraternity hazing because it involves screaming at and belittling cadets, then moving them to the gym to try and break them physically. Cadets engage in an unwinnable floor workout until their arms and legs give out. The workout continues until the fittest cadet drops from exhaustion. Once this workout is complete, the cadets are brought to the front of the gym to roll around like pieces of bacon, while the PT staff call them pigs. Once the time in the gym is through, cadets are treated to a run around the academy grounds. The run is called the "rabbit run" because in the old days, before some cadets actually started complaining, the PT staff would run the cadets until they threw up and fed the rabbits. Randy Atchison collapsed and died in 201 following one of these CHP academy workouts. His cause of death was rhabdomyolysis and severe dehydration.

Rhabdomyolysis is a breakdown of muscle tissue, releasing dangerous substances into the bloodstream, associated with excessive physical activity, often in combination with dehydration. (Ayoob, 1012)

Sergeant Gomez ran the PT program when I was in the academy. He had a reputation for being overly cruel to cadets, in a manner that wouldn't be tolerated now because it was hazing. There were stories of him making cadets do pushups into piles of mud and dangling a candy bar on a fishing line over the pull-up bars to tease overweight cadets. My run-in with Gomez came during a day when my class was doing several hundred sit-ups. Being on antibiotics I was having stomach issues and thought I was going to poop myself because my stomach hurt so bad. This resulted in me letting out a silent but deadly fart, which made the entire area smell. Gomez quickly picked up on the smell and demanded someone admit to it or the whole class would suffer. Having integrity, which the CHP claimed they required, I took ownership and spent the next almost two hours being physically and mentally tortured by the PT staff.

After completing three floor workouts and a run, I was told to return to the gym. I was told to place my back against a wall in a seated position, which is affectionately called the electric chair. While in this position two staff members took turns yelling at me for farting, while another threw a basketball at the wall next to my head over and over again. If you've ever wondered why so many CHP officers are unfriendly and angry, well now you know. Gomez was an unnecessarily cruel bully who should have never been allowed to haze cadets, let alone wear a badge.

Following my run-in with Gomez, I was placed on "double" physical training for four months. I was in decent shape, but I finally left the academy due to an injury that resulted from the stress on my body. I would go through several doctors while waiting for an official diagnosis before being reclassified to dispatcher. I have a ton of respect for the job dispatchers do, but it was terrible. I will never forget taking a 911 call from a father whose child was unresponsive. He was screaming and crying. All I could do is transfer him to the fire department. When I needed an out, my former employer had an opening, so I returned to McGeorge.

While working for McGeorge in 2010, I landed my first interview with the lottery after sending in several applications. I was so excited when I got the letter from the lottery stating I was being selected to interview. I drove to a beat-down office building located behind a strip club in the industrial section of Sacramento. I would later find out the building was constructed in just a few months because of the push to get the lottery operational in 1985. I interviewed with Lieutenant Helen Brean and John Tristant. I thought I nailed the interview but ultimately didn't get selected because I didn't have academy certification. Over the next several years, I applied every time I saw an open position.

I recognized that one of the issues I had with this interview was going up against individuals who already had a law enforcement academy certificate. This made me realize I had to take action. Having left the CHP academy due to an injury and realizing that getting someone to hire me to go through an academy would be an uphill battle, I knew I had to find a way to make it happen.

In 2011, I decided to pay to put myself through an extended law enforcement academy at a local community college. The academy staff mostly worked for the local police department academies during the day, so I would get the same education so to speak. It took me almost a year going to the academy three nights a week and all day on Saturday. I was also working full-time for McGeorge and was sometimes working forty-eight hours a week. I was appointed to a class leadership position and graduated with a class of twenty-eight recruits. The academy training was the equivalent of an associate's degree and would give me a leg-up on other applicants. I had finally settled on a career and was putting all of my eggs in one basket.

Completing the academy was one of the most difficult things I ever did. 2012 was the same year that multiple police departments laid off officers and prison realignment took place in California, meaning prisoners being released into various counties. The counties didn't have the staff to properly supervise the recently released inmates, or assist them, which resulted in increased criminal activity around the law school. One of the most important things I did during my law enforcement career happened at McGeorge that year. An older guy and a younger girl were wandering around the campus. At one point, a staff member believed the girl had stolen a camera from their bag. My partner and I then began searching the campus for the pair, eventually finding them in the law library computer lab. The fight was on when I approached the male and asked him if he was a student. He stood up and attempted to shove me, at which point we slammed each other around the computer lab while several law students looked on in horror. My partner and I got him in handcuffs, and additional officers from local jurisdictions showed up after the fact.

Initially, I believed he fought with us because of the missing camera. It turned out the girl was fifteen and was a missing person from Connecticut. The guy was thirty-six years old and had been pimping her out. He had been using the law school's computer lab to set up her dates for several weeks. He was also a "nonviolent" offender who was released early because his most recent arrest was a burglary charge, even though the previous ones involved victimizing minors.

The fight was one of several I would have that year while trying to juggle work, academy, and personal relationships. Although it was grueling, I eventually graduated and received my academy certification. I started applying for departments to take the next step in my career and applied for the lottery again.

In May of 2013, I got another chance to interview with the lottery.

I got the call while attending my nephew Connor's middle school graduation in San Diego. I was extremely excited to have an opportunity to interview. I annoyed my family and my girlfriend by talking about it nonstop. I showed them the *Dateline* videos and talked about how badly I wanted the job.

I drove to the same location behind the strip club in the same industrial area. This time, I was greeted by a beautiful six-story building with the big sunburst logo on the top. The old building had been torn down and replaced with a parking lot. I arrived for my interview armed with a binder full of my accomplishments and reasons for why I should get the job.

I interviewed with Brean, who had been promoted to acting deputy director since my first interview, and Steve Olsen, who was a lieutenant. I spent days preparing for the interview and came prepared to leave with a job offer. I had the perfect answers to all of their questions and even incorporated the mission statement of SLED into some of my answers. In closing, I told Brean she would have to hire me eventually because I was going to keep coming back until she got sick of seeing me. It worked.

On October 22, 2013, I was sworn in as a California Lottery SLED investigator after going through a background investigation, psychological exam, medical exam, and other testing. I was twenty-nine years old, being issued a take-home car, brand new office, BlackBerry cell phone, and raid vest. The raid vest looked like something your grandfather would wear while he was fishing. It was fishnet with pockets for all of my police equipment and said "Police" across the top with "California State Lottery" written below in large white letters. I thought this was the coolest thing ever because it reminded me of the *X-Files* when Mulder and Scully would put on their raid vests and kick in doors announcing themselves as federal agents. I also got to wear plain clothes to work and wouldn't have to wear a uniform for the foreseeable future.

I was sworn in by Paula LaBrie, who was the acting deputy director of the lottery. I raised my right hand and took the oath of office in front of my mom, girlfriend, friends, and the lottery staff. I truly felt like I was at home and had finally made it to where I wanted to be. In a way, I didn't feel like I deserved this job because I hadn't been a detective who had retired and was looking for a second career. I was a kid who Brean decided to take a chance on because, as she told my mom and girlfriend, I was "tenacious." This made me feel accomplished and humbled at the same time. That day, I promised myself I would work harder than anyone else, learn everything I needed to learn, and prove myself in everything I did. There was no doubt in my mind that could do the job, and do it well.

CHAPTER 3

Learning the Ropes

Investigator Geno Davis started with me at the lottery on the same day. Davis had been working for the state for almost twenty years in various positions. He had come from the Consumer Affairs Dentist Bureau where he was a sworn investigator who carried a gun. I was amazed to know that dentists were dangerous, but then I remembered the dentist from *Little Shop of Horrors*, so it was a possibility. Davis was the typical government yes-man who didn't want to rock the boat. He enjoyed having an easy state job.

Our training officer/mentor was Investigator Amber Bettar, who had worked for the lottery for several years as a civilian before being put through an academy by SLED. Amber and I had actually crossed paths a few times while going through the academy because our academies were at the same facility. She was going through the city police academy during the day while I was attending the extended evening academy at night. She was attractive, funny, and could outshoot anyone. She had a degree in forensics and could have been fast-tracked to any agency she wanted to work for. She stayed with the lottery because she was a dedicated single mother who made her daughter a top priority.

Amber trained us on the multiple lottery systems, conducting background investigations, SLED policies, and lottery regulations. The mission of SLED was to ensure the honesty, integrity, and fairness of the operation of California's lottery. This was engrained in me on my first day as I was introduced to the amount of detail that went into ensuring the rightful owner of a ticket was paid and that lottery retail locations were being honest. Everything SLED did was rooted in the Lottery Act and lottery regulations. These rules were fairly self-explanatory in that they were exactly what you would expect from a gambling establishment, which just so happened to be government-run. The major difference between a casino and the lottery was the fact that the house didn't always win, and when it did—the house was public education.

I'm a fairly simple guy when it comes to law enforcement. Prior to starting with the lottery, my philosophy was *see bad guy, watch bad guy do bad thing, and arrest bad guy*. After arresting the bad guy, I would write a lengthy report explaining why. SLED was the most sophisticated law enforcement agency I had ever worked for. All lottery tickets were part of individually numbered games. Each individual ticket had a unique serial number, which could be researched through the lottery's computer systems. The computer systems tracked all of the movements of the tickets. The system could track what retailer the tickets were assigned to, how much they were worth, the retail cost of each ticket, and where the ticket was checked to see if it was a winner or loser.

I found the online games to be the most fascinating because of the amount of information available for each ticket. Online games involve computer-generated tickets such as Powerball, where the tickets are generated from a printer attached to a lottery computer. The lottery has the ability to pinpoint the location where the ticket was sold, the exact date/time the ticket was generated, and how the numbers for the game were selected. Online games have two methods for play. The customer can manually select their numbers for each drawing, or they can have the computer randomly select the numbers (Remember Eddie Tipton?). The lottery is aware of this information once a winning ticket has been identified. Depending on the public interest, the lottery may immediately put out a press release that identifies the location where the winning ticket was sold and the winning numbers.

The information for the winning ticket is sent to the lieutenant who supervises the region where the winning ticket was sold. The lieutenant assigns the case to an investigator, who responds to the location and obtains information including surveillance footage of the potential purchase. Surveillance footage can be obtained if the retail location has a surveillance system and updates the date/time stamp. The lottery didn't require its retail owners to have operational surveillance systems and had no requirement for the information to be current. Oftentimes, this results in an Investigator having to spend hours with a system trying to guess when a winning ticket was sold or just giving up because the time stamp is off by too many days. Some retail locations still use VHS tapes, while others just have cameras up to serve as a deterrent. This is a major point of contention amongst investigators because it greatly impacts their ability to identify the rightful owner of a winning ticket. The lottery will also notify the retail owner when a large winning ticket is sold and will respond to the location with an oversized check prior to SLED being able to respond to the location and obtain the required information.

This was troubling to many investigators because it hurt the integrity of an investigation, especially for a winning ticket for a large cash prize. This led to situations where retail owners would be on the lookout for the winning ticket so they could take it for themselves, which was the case at a Camarillo, CA convenience store in 2006. Bob Sehested took his winning ticket to the Crossroads Market and Liquor to check his ticket to see if it was a winner. The owner, Sam Grair, had already been notified by the lottery that the winning ticket had been sold at his store, so he was waiting for the winner to stop by. When Sehested gave the ticket to Grair to check, he took the winning ticket from Sehested and switched it with his ticket, which was worth a few dollars. Grair attempted to claim the prize for the ticket. Grair couldn't answer questions investigators asked about the ticket. Luckily the store's surveillance system actually worked and the rightful owner was located. Grair was arrested for the theft and was ultimately convicted. The situation didn't change the manner in which the lottery made its notifications, so the same crime could be committed today. (Wolowicz, 2006)

Oftentimes, the news media would respond to the location where a winning ticket was sold. They interviewed store employees and customers about the ticket. The lottery would occasionally have an investigator on call to respond to the location and obtain the information when the prize created a media buzz, but this was the exception, not the rule. The location where the ticket is sold is still disclosed to the general public and the retail location before the investigator has a chance to respond and get the information. This was the case when a winning ticket for over $500 million was sold in Chino Hills, CA. Hundreds of people and multiple news vans were present at the location when the investigator arrived. He turned around and left without even trying to get surveillance footage.

Not having surveillance footage is problematic because the lottery regulations allow players to claim prizes without having the physical ticket "if" they can provide "substantial proof" that they are the lawful owner of the missing ticket. In theory, this would require some sort of tangible evidence on the part of the claimant that satisfies the lottery's confidential validation procedures. These procedures rely heavily on ticket information, surveillance footage, and the physical ticket. This is why obtaining surveillance video is so important when investigating a claim. The footage is the best tool at the disposal of the lottery but not the only one. Surveillance footage and photographs are compared to the individual who is claiming the ticket. There have been multiple occasions where the surveillance footage has proven the individual who is claiming a ticket isn't the rightful owner. This was the case with the incident involving Sehested.

Just like a scratch-off ticket, online tickets receive a serial number, but the online tickets also have the date and time-stamped when they are printed. This provides a level of security for the lawful owner of a winning ticket. Requiring retail locations to scan scratch-off tickets as they're sold to document the date/time in the same manner was suggested many times by SLED to lottery management. The suggestion made sense because the lottery can't track the date/time a scratch-off ticket is sold in the same manner. The suggestion was ignored, which continued to leave investigators with nothing more than the statements provided by claimants when a questionable or big winning scratch-off ticket was claimed.

As I processed all of this information, it became apparent there were many flaws with the lottery, which I wouldn't have expected from a government agency, especially one that was responsible for such a large amount of public money. When investigators questioned issues, we were constantly told that certain changes could affect sales and the retailers wouldn't want to do more work. Senior investigators would tell me that things changed for the worse once Paula LaBrie became the acting deputy director of the lottery. She wasn't a fan of SLED because she believed the work of the investigators hurt sales, as arrests and potential lawsuits for denied claims exposed bigger issues. This didn't matter, though, because SLED management encouraged us to continue doing the right thing.

After working for the lottery for a few months I got into my groove and was in a constant state of learning. I would handle several background investigations each week. The Lottery Act requires background investigations of all potential employees, contractors, and vendors. The worst of these were disclosure investigations because they required an investigation into a company that could include individuals residing in different states—or even different countries. The only exception to these detailed investigations was when they were personal friends or former employers of lottery management.

Investigators were also required to help answer phone calls from the general public. The calls included lottery retailers calling in stolen tickets, law enforcement requesting assistance, and players reporting suspicious activity at lottery retail locations. The worst calls came from retail owners and clerks reporting stolen tickets. Some stores will have thousands of dollars' worth of scratch-off tickets assigned to their business. The lottery doesn't require stores to keep an inventory, so when the retail owner didn't have the information for the stolen tickets, I would have to go through every scratch-off ticket pack they had in their possession. This could sometimes take hours and involve call-backs from the retail owner saying they reported the wrong tickets as stolen.

One of my favorite callers was Shawn Hayes, who began calling the lottery shortly after I started. Hayes claimed he was arrested for domestic violence and had purchased a winning lottery ticket right before he was taken to jail. While in jail, his father married his ex-girlfriend and assumed Hayes' identity. He claimed the ticket he had purchased was worth "millions" and he was the rightful owner. It would take Hayes about twenty minutes to get to his theft allegation. He would tell me how his father and ex-girlfriend were living in this amazing compound he couldn't get into. They knew he was the winner and would constantly tease him when he was at the compound, which he had just said he couldn't get into.

Now me being a new guy I believed there was a potential case here, so I conducted a thorough investigation. I obtained the names of all of the involved parties and began conducting searches through all of the lottery's systems. I found absolutely nothing and quickly realized Hayes was either fabricating the story or was delusional. When I first discussed my findings, I handled him gently and explained all of the steps I had taken to investigate his claim. Hayes refused to listen and continued calling every day for months. After he was told to stop calling SLED, he would call in and use a fake name. He would tell a completely different story before going back to the same one he had originally given. I was finally able to stop the calls after getting his probation officer to incorporate a non-contact clause in his probation terms.

Hayes was one of many callers who believed they were entitled to millions of dollars. Some of the callers were angry; some were sad. I had been in several fights as a police officer where I had to use force to subdue someone I was arresting. In most cases, the suspect would end up thanking me for arresting them because I would take the time to explain to them why I had to use force, talking to them like a human being. I never received a single complaint about excessive force and was never threatened with violence, or a lawsuit. Early on, I lost count of the number of lottery callers who said they were going to sue me, kill me, or have me fired. None of them followed, though.

CHAPTER 4

My First Big Case

A new deputy director was appointed by the governor in November of 2014. Stephen Tacchini was a former assistant chief with the San Francisco Police Department and had worked in law enforcement for over twenty years. Tacchini was very approachable and took a passive stance at first while learning how the lottery operated. He was very calculated in everything he did. When he wanted to change something, he approached things head-on and didn't deflect by saying someone else was making him do it.

The headquarters division of SLED assigned one investigator each day to stay in the building until five. One afternoon, I was working with my lieutenant when someone from Corporate Communications came downstairs to report an issue they were extremely concerned about. They were contacted by a concerned lottery player who received a message through their social media account on *Facebook*. The individual was contacted by a person who identified themself as a lottery agent and had the same name as a Supreme Court justice. The lottery agent informed the player they had won a large lottery prize and they needed to pay a processing fee in order to claim their prize. The lottery agent informed the player they could pay the processing fee by obtaining a money card they could purchase at a retail store.

This type of fraud is common throughout the United States and costs victims billions of dollars each year. The scammers will contact their victims identifying themselves as a representative of a government agency such as a state lottery, a county court, or the Internal Revenue Services. The scammer then convinces the victim they need to pay some sort of a fee associated with the scam. The victim is instructed to utilize a service such as Western Union or Green Dot Money to pay the fee, which is sent to the "representative" of the government agency. Most of the time, the "representative" is based out of a Nigerian office, but occasionally the victim will be instructed to pay a representative, who is a money mule, located in the United States. The scams are intricate and usually prey on the elderly.

Corporate Communications was concerned about how this issue could affect the reputation of the lottery because the individual was identifying themselves as a California lottery agent. When Corporate Communications went to the *Facebook* page, they found an exact replica of the official California Lottery *Facebook* page. The individual identified themself as a lottery agent and was contacting individuals who were following the actual California lottery page.

My lieutenant, Ray Gutierrez, and I went to Tacchini's office to brief him on the complaint from the executive floor. Tacchini informed us he wanted a thorough investigation into the creator of the page to determine if any lottery players had been victims. He wanted an investigator to write a search warrant to obtain all of the information on who established the account and how long it had been operational. Gutierrez and I exited Tacchini's office. He smiled, patted me on the back, and said he was assigning the investigation to me. It was his smile that concerned me the most.

I returned to my office and sat in my chair, proceeding to stare at my computer screen for several minutes. I had only written one search warrant in my entire career and had no idea what I was supposed to write to get the information I needed. I didn't feel comfortable telling Gutierrez I was in over my head, and I felt the pressure of needing to impress Tacchini. I used every single resource I had at my disposal and found a friend who had previously written a search warrant for a *Facebook* account. The warrant I wrote contained all of the information I needed to include. Because I wanted to be as thorough as possible, I included screenshots, comparisons, and pictures. I took my warrant to the Judge and got complimented on the content. After getting the Judge's signature, I returned to work feeling a huge sense of accomplishment. I had no idea that I has just opened a huge can of worms.

After sending the search warrant to *Facebook* and having to go back to the courts multiple times to get an extension on my warrant, I received a huge file containing hundreds of pages of messages and log-on information. While I was unable to identify any actual victims who had sent money, I was able to get a phone number that had been sent to several victims. The phone number was associated with another *Facebook* page for an attractive woman whose page was filled with photos of her partying and wearing revealing clothes. The internet protocol (IP) addresses for the computers that accessed the account were primarily located in Nigeria. One IP address was located in Florida, which was promising because it meant there was possibly a suspect who was in the United States. I wrote another search warrant and received another file, which contained several hundred pages worth of messages and photographs.

As I began reading the messages, I noticed the account holder had been contacting men in countless countries. Each of the men was contacted by the account holder who initiated a conversation telling them some version of the same story about her looking for love through *Facebook*. The scammer started with minor flirting, then would start asking them for money after telling them they were stuck in Nigeria and had to make payments to the government.

I located a victim who lived in San Francisco, CA, who was deep in the scam. I read several message threads that involved the scammer telling the victim how much they loved them and how they wanted to return to the Bay Area so the two could be together. The scammer told the victim they were stuck in Nigeria after a vacation. They said the Nigerian government was extremely corrupt and was keeping her passport so she couldn't return. The government officials were willing to bargain if she would pay them, but she had no access to her money because the government confiscated her bank cards and identification. The victim continued to wire money to various "government officials" who were accepting the cash in exchange for letting the scammer return to the United States. The San Francisco victim continued to send money to Nigeria using Western Union. Despite moments of clarity, he would still send additional money because it seemed he truly believed she was in love with him.

As I continued scrolling through the message logs, I almost had a heart attack when I saw a nude woman with her vagina on full display. The photographs got more graphic, and I realized I should probably go have a chat with the lieutenant who was responsible for monitoring computer usage at the lottery. It was an awkward conversation because he was staring intently at the nude photographs while looking back at me in a way that made me feel like I was in the principal's office. I provided him with the specifics of my investigation and explained why the nude woman was in my usage log. The lieutenant told me not to worry about it, and feel free to bring more photographs by his office I got "any more good ones." It was kind of like having "the talk" with your parents.

After reviewing account details, I found the same IP address accessing the account several times in Florida, which was my first big lead. My next course of action was obtaining a warrant for the phone number associated with both *Facebook* accounts. After writing and serving several more search warrants, I was finally able to associate the phone number with a Google Voice account.

Google Voice is one of the best tools for perpetrating fraud I have ever seen. A person can establish a Google Voice account and disguise their phone number using an area code from any city in the entire world. This means a person in Nigeria can establish a Google Voice account and select an area code from San Diego, CA that will show up when they call you. Google Voice is even nice enough to erase your call and text history every thirty days so there is no evidence of what you are doing if law enforcement identifies the number as part of an investigation. The only nice thing about the service is that you usually have to set up the account using a legitimate phone number, which was the case with my suspect.

After several more search warrants, I was able to identify a suspect who resided in Florida. He had several prior convictions for fraud and identity theft and resided a few blocks away from the IP address at a library that was logging onto the *Facebook* account. The number was associated with three different *Facebook* accounts, including the fake lottery account. I finally had all of the information I needed but was pretty sure I wouldn't be able to travel to Florida to interrogate my bad guy. The only solution, which would also allow me to close my case, was to refer it to a federal law enforcement agency.

After several weeks of playing phone tag, I was able to secure a meeting with the Sacramento office of the Federal Bureau of Investigation, or the FBI as all *X-Files* fans know them. I was truly excited about this amazing career opportunity. I saw no way I could lose considering I had a stateside suspect and a stateside victim. I had already served ten search warrants related to the case and had a huge packet of evidence, so this was going to be easy. I had a cramped meeting in my office with three special agents.

One of the FBI agents I spoke with told me about Nigeria and how big of a business fraud is in the country. There are "Internet cafes" all over the place, which are basically pop-up tents with card tables. Scammers sit at the tables 24/7, make phone calls, send blanket emails, and text unsuspecting victims in the United States. Each of the cafes has Western Union, and other money transfer businesses, which facilitate the payments to the scammers. While the United States does have law enforcement personnel in place to investigate some of these crimes, according to the agent, the Nigerian government will only take enforcement action when a predetermined amount is taken from a victim in the United States. The unfortunate thing is this amount is usually well beyond the average life savings of a retiree, so they have no chance of recovering their losses if they fall victim to a scam. This broke my heart.

After talking about these scams and the fact that I had a suspect who was in the United States, we got down to business. I presented my case to the FBI agents as if I was a car salesman trying to get a commission. I gave them a victim, I gave them a suspect, and I gave them hundreds of pages of legally acquired evidence. I almost did a victory dance when they agreed to take the case and run with it. I shook their hands and gave them my packet. The disposition of my case was "referred to outside agency," which everyone in my office knew was the FBI. I was proud because months of hard work paid off in the form of me giving a case to Feds. The only problem was that the Feds don't always play well with others. I was never told what the outcome of my investigation was because they never returned my calls. Tacchini and my lieutenant were pleased, but I got no closure. I'm still bothered as much by this today as I was then because I'm nosy and want to know what happened.

CHAPTER 5

Terrible Commute

In early 2014, it was discovered that the lottery and the company that maintained all of the systems used to produce and validate lottery tickets had overlooked a major requirement of the Lottery Act. California's Lottery Act and lottery regulations require a background investigation of every potential employee, contractor, and vendor who will receive money from the lottery. Due to an oversight, the lottery hadn't conducted a background investigation into any of the call center employees who assisted lottery retailers or the repairmen who serviced lottery retail locations on the border for almost two years. This meant that people who were trusted with information specific to the operation of California's lottery hadn't been properly vetted and were actively working on accounts. This caused alarm because the lottery had experienced breeches by vendors in the past. An incident involving someone who hadn't received a background investigation would create scrutiny for the lottery.

Two security guards employed by Plant Protection, the security company that guarded lottery offices, were arrested in 1985 for stealing lottery computer programs. The guards stole various programs, manuals, and other operational documents in an effort to locate where winning tickets would be sold. The lottery also had an employee from their prize payments department intercept a winning $5,000 scratch-off ticket. She removed the name of the winner who had mailed the winning ticket to lottery headquarters. She and her cousin worked together to separately claim the ticket and deposited the funds into her personal bank account. (Ferrell, 1989) (Unknown, 2 Lottery workers charged in computer theft, 1985)

The solution to this problem was to throw money at it by having investigators handle multiple background investigations at once, which would be done during non-business hours. This meant several late nights at headquarters collecting overtime to correct the issue before something happened. My partners and I spent several long evenings conducting phone interviews, reviewing background packets, and running information.

After one of these long evenings, I decided it was finally time to go home. I had been issued a vehicle that was equipped with emergency lights and a siren but didn't have a police radio. I didn't really care because I only had to drive one freeway exit to get to my apartment, and what could possibly happen in such a short distance? I got in my car and started toward the freeway. I drove past the sketchy strip club located at the front of the lottery parking lot and turned onto the freeway onramp. As I began picking up speed, a disheveled-looking guy jumped in front of my car. I swerved around him and immediately looked in my rearview mirror. I saw him try to jump in front of another vehicle and realized he was actually trying to commit suicide.

At this moment, I realized it would be a great time for me to have a radio to notify a dispatcher there was an issue and I needed help. I called 911 and continued toward my exit, which was only about twenty-five feet away. As I described the matter to the dispatcher, I began thinking about my relationship to the situation. I'm a sworn peace officer who is driving an emergency vehicle with lights and sirens. *I'm currently reporting a suicidal subject who is jumping in front of vehicles on Interstate 5. This call is being recorded. If he decides to jump in front of a minivan carrying a family that swerves and crashes into the American River, I'll be that asshole cop who did nothing.* I wasn't that type of person.

I flipped on my lights and siren, and I made an extremely unsafe U-turn back onto the freeway. I continued talking to the dispatcher in my headset as I flew down the freeway trying to get back to the onramp before the guy killed himself or someone else. As I cleared the intersection and returned to the onramp, I saw him standing on the shoulder of the freeway. I drove up the onramp with my lights and siren blaring. As I slowed down, the guy jumped in front of my car again. This pissed me off and was a little surprising. After realizing he wasn't going to be able to use my car to end his life, the guy started walking away on the shoulder.

I exited my vehicle while the dispatcher was screaming at me to stay in my car. I calmly—well, sort of calmly—explained that I was a lottery cop and knew what I was doing, which I kind of did. The dispatcher said they were sorry for yelling at me and asked if I would stay on the line. I screamed, "Police! Get on the ground." Much to my surprise, he listened to me and laid down on his stomach. He was sobbing and talking incoherently while I placed him in handcuffs. I told him I was going to get him help and placed him in the back seat of my car. I asked the dispatcher to contact local law enforcement to assist me because I really had no idea what to do with a person who wanted to kill themself and couldn't leave him in the back of my car.

As I was reversing down the onramp and praying I didn't get hit by a careless idiot driving at a high rate of speed, he began talking. He told me he was distraught because he found out his girlfriend was cheating on him. They were homeless, so she was truly all he had and he didn't know how to deal with the pain. I opened up to him about having a girlfriend cheat on me, and I told him it just wasn't worth it. He seemed to calm down a little but continued to sob, which really did break my heart. There is something to be said about being so distraught that you just didn't want to deal with life anymore, and not everyone understands it. This was the first time I had actually dealt with someone actively trying to take their own life, and considering some of the horror stories I had heard, this went as well as it could have.

As we neared the main street at the bottom of the onramp, I noticed a marked police cruiser at the stoplight. I hit my siren to get their attention and pulled into a nearby gas station. The cruiser followed me into the station and asked me if I was alright. I told him about my passenger and asked him if he could assist me. He informed me he was a reserve officer but would get some officers to me right away. We discussed my job and why I was working late while we waited for his partners to arrive. After several minutes, three additional cars arrived. I told the officers what the subject had done and the statements he had made to me before they arrived. They swapped out the handcuffs and placed him in the back of one of their cars.

I gave one of the officers my statement and returned to my car. As I got ready to leave, I looked in my rearview mirror and saw an officer removing the handcuffs from my suicidal subject. The subject walked into the darkness, and the officers left the area before I could ask anyone why. I had worked in law enforcement for several years by now, so I knew the officers simply did not want to deal with the paperwork associated with an involuntary hold of a person who was a danger to himself. I was pissed off but knew there could have been other pressing calls and arguing with them for being incompetent was a losing battle. Unfortunately, this wasn't an uncommon occurrence, so it wouldn't have done me any good to track down supervisors. I drove home, feeling angry and sad about what had occurred.

I notified supervisors by telephone about what had happened and was assured they would make the appropriate notifications. I was a little nervous the next day because I wasn't sure how Tacchini was going to feel about my actions. I was a lottery investigator and not a street cop. Everyone knew what had happened by the time I walked through the door because cops gossip more than the members of a small town. Davis immediately told me to come to his office and close the door. He told me I had done the right thing but I probably should have just called it in. He said he had worked for other state agencies who would fire an Investigator for what I did because I was off duty, and told me to be careful in the future. Considering I had only worked for the lottery for a few months, I was a little panicked but also pissed off that someone who was a "peace officer" would tell me to just let someone die. I went to my office and began contemplating how I was going to be released during probation, and what other employment opportunities may be

40

available for someone like me.

About an hour later, Tacchini and Brean walked into my office. I expected the worst considering everything Davis had just told me. Tacchini walked up to my desk and extended his hand. As I shook it, he told me I had done a great job and he was proud of me. I breathed a sigh of relief and went over to Davis' office to rub it in his face. I told him what Tacchini had said and told him he was an asshole. He laughed, told me he was surprised, and believed this organization was going to be different from the ones he had previously worked for. I agreed.

CHAPTER 6

Mega Millions

In December of 2013, the Mega Millions jackpot grew to over $636 million, which was one of the largest jackpots in lottery history. One of the LED jackpot signs was right outside of my office, so it was a little fun to walk out and see the huge numbers for the game. Two winning tickets were eventually sold, one of which was in California. The winning ticket from California was sold at a lottery retail location in San Jose, CA, and was worth $324 million. An investigator was sent to the location to obtain surveillance footage, which was normal protocol. The location didn't have an operational surveillance system, which sent the lottery into a little bit of a panic, given all the media attention.

While all of this was occurring, I was asked to participate in a retailer compliance program operation in San Francisco, CA. This was the first time I got to work one of these operations and was going to be the undercover Investigator, so I was super excited. I met with two great investigators, Todd Kyle and Dennis Maffei, who filled me in on how the operation worked and shared some funny stories about what they had done in the past to look more like regular customers. Maffei told me he would sometimes act drunk and stumble into a location just to see what the clerk would do. Usually, the clerk would steal his ticket because they believed he was too drunk to know he had a winner.

We went to several locations that all did the right thing and told me my decoy ticket was a winner. I decided to switch things up and act like a drunk customer. After stumbling into a 7-Eleven, I almost smacked my face on the door because it was locked. I gave my ticket to the clerk who promptly congratulated me on my thousand-dollar winning ticket. Staying in character, I exited the store and stumbled across the street into a small liquor store. The clerk was on the phone and seemed completely disinterested in me. I walked up to the counter and handed her my winning decoy ticket. I asked her to check it for me and walked over to the gummy candy rack because I saw one of my favorites. I grabbed the bag and returned to the clerk who was still talking on the phone. She checked the ticket on the lottery computer and placed the phone on the counter. She told me I had won $5 and grabbed the cash from a cigar box. She handed me the $5, I paid for my gummy candy and returned to Maffei's car. As I exited the store, I was excited because this was the first time I had been working undercover for the lottery and the first time I'd had a decoy ticket stolen from me.

Maffei and Kyle knew the clerk stole the tickets from me because I was wearing a body wire. I was also wearing a ridiculous hidden camera in the form of an oversized Bluetooth headset. The headset was extremely bulky and it looked like I was wearing a video game headset. The size of the headset didn't seem to matter though because the clerk was distracted by stealing what she believed was a $1,000 winning ticket from an unsuspecting customer. I quickly gave the recording device to

Kyle, who downloaded it onto his computer to secure the footage as evidence.

Maffei's phone rang a few minutes later. It was Lieutenant Tristant, who informed Maffei someone had checked the winning $348 million ticket at a market in San Francisco's China Town. This was important because the store that sold the winning ticket didn't have an operational surveillance system, so this video could be the only way to identify the rightful owner. We quickly drove across town and arrived at the location. It took us several minutes to find a parking space because the area was packed.

We went inside the location and showed our police credentials to three different employees who didn't speak English. We were finally able to convince them to call the owner, who showed up twenty minutes later. We told the owner why we were there and asked him if we could review the store's surveillance system. He agreed.

The manager escorted us to the back of the store. We walked down a long corridor with warehouse-style shelves stacked floor to ceiling. We had to duck under one of the shelves to go through a small space that led to the store's office. I almost decapitated myself getting inside.

The four of us watched the video and observed a family walk up to the counter holding several lottery tickets. An older man handed the clerk a ticket, which the clerk checked on the lottery computer. The clerk handed him a yellow piece of paper that displayed the value of the winning ticket. He showed the receipt to his young daughter, who began jumping up and down. He motioned for her to stop, which she immediately did. He took the ticket, folded it in half, and placed it in his wallet. He placed his wallet in his back pocket and exited the store into a large crowd of people. I couldn't stop myself as I yelled, "You idiot" because he had a folded piece of paper in his wallet worth millions and just walked into a large crowd of people.

A few days later, I was working at headquarters when the ticket arrived at the office for validation. It still had the crease across the middle from where he had folded it in the store. I briefly held the ticket in my hand because I had never touched anything worth so much money. In that moment, I couldn't help but imagine how this man's life and the life of his family were going to change forever. I also thought about how scary it was to know that the only thing that stood between joy and tragedy was the clerk at the store. This moment made me proud to be a part of the lottery, but also made me realize how important my job was because of how close this man could have been to losing out on something so amazing.

CHAPTER 7

Auditors

Someone submitted a claim for the prize about a month after the clerk stole the decoy scratch-off ticket from me in San Francisco. The person who claimed the ticket was an elderly woman who provided the same address as the clerk who stole the ticket from me. The claim was mailed to the lottery and wasn't claimed in person at a lottery office, so nobody verified the identity of the person claiming the ticket. Had the ticket not been a decoy, it would have been paid with no questions asked because there was nothing on the claim form that made it appear suspicious. All of the boxes that asked if the person claiming the prize was a lottery retail owner or related to one were checked "no."

The clerk who stole the ticket from me ended up being the owner of the store. I researched her name and known associates. Her husband had claimed several tickets worth a few thousand dollars and was paid with no investigation, despite sharing the same address. I was surprised by this, considering the owner's husband listed her address on his claim form. The lottery claim system hadn't identified him as being related to a lottery retail owner, even though he was clearly married to one. I asked one of my lieutenants how something like this could happen.

I was told that the lottery didn't have a system in place to flag addresses or other claimant information when a claim was entered into the lottery's database. The system could be changed to make this type of notification, but it would be time-consuming for the employees who enter the information. The lottery wanted to ensure that customers were paid as quickly as possible and didn't want the added burden of researching the individual claiming a prize unless it was over $250,000.

When a player claims a ticket worth $600 or more with the lottery, they are required to fill out a claim form. The form asks for general information about the claimant, including their name, contact information, and citizenship status. The form also asks the claimant to disclose if they are a lottery retail owner, employed by a lottery retail owner, or related to a lottery retail owner. The assumption is that the claimant will answer all of the questions truthfully because they have to sign the claim form under penalty of perjury.

The claim form is mailed to lottery headquarters by the person who is claiming it or by the district office where the person claims the ticket in person. The claim is entered into the lottery's claim database by a prize payments employee who enters the information into the system line by line. The lottery doesn't set up the system to flag certain information such as addresses or previous claims, even though it has the ability to do so. The information is instead entered by the prize payments employee based on what the claimant wrote on the claim form.

A claimant who discloses their ownership of a lottery retail business on the first claim they submit won't be flagged as a retail owner when they submit a second claim and lie to save time by answering "no" to all of the lottery retailer questions. The system doesn't tell the prize payments employee the claimant is a retail owner if the claimant stops checking the appropriate box after their first claim. Because of this flaw in the system, there are countless claimants in the lottery's claim database who have several different profiles and player numbers, most of which are lottery retail owners.

There was no way I could be the only person who noticed a significant problem with the lottery. It was my belief that this system allowed for a large amount of fraud, considering the fact that the lottery only investigated claims with a cash prize value of $250,000 or more. While my primary concern was the potential victimization of lottery customers, I also saw the potential for other crimes such as money laundering. In theory, an individual who is operating a convenience store could rack up hundreds of thousands of dollars in stolen prizes by simply not checking a box and claiming multiple prizes as long as the value was under the threshold. I shared my concerns with Lieutenant Derek Beverly, who was a retired captain from the California Department of Motor Vehicles.

Beverly was an expert in data mining and had been assigned to a federal task force to identify terrorist organizations. One of Beverly's major accomplishments was identifying one of the masterminds behind the terrorist attack on September 11, 2001. He identified the individual by linking their identity to those of the hijackers based on the date and location where their California driver's licenses had been printed.

Beverly conducted my background investigation prior to my being hired by the lottery. He considered me his protégé and took steps to connect me with the right people and provide me with opportunities to make a name for myself. Beverly also believed there was a significant amount of money laundering and fraud occurring within the lottery. Beverly was concerned this money was being funneled to terrorist organizations. His views weren't popular, so his attempts to develop a task force to track potential fraud and abnormal winning patterns were denied by lottery management on multiple occasions.

In early 2014, Beverly was asked to provide a presentation to the California Association of Fraud Auditors. Roberto Zavala, the chief auditor for the lottery, was one of the members of the executive board. Beverly asked me to present a brief case study on the lottery *Facebook* case I had investigated. Beverly and I met with Zavala and showed him our power point presentation.

Zavala was impressed and asked me if I had noticed any potential issues with the lottery as a new employee. I told him about my case in San Francisco and the discovery that the retail owner's husband wasn't properly flagged in the lottery's claim system. I told Zavala my concern was the amount of potential fraud being allowed by the lottery because of the number of claims being paid that were under $250,000 with no investigation. Millions of dollars of public education money was being paid each year without a second look.

I told Zavala that after a few months of entering claims into the system myself, I noticed the process was flawed and time-consuming. The claim system was a computer program that was smart enough to identify winning tickets based on the ticket serial number, so a simple programming change could increase output and help identify questionable claims. The only major change would be to have some sort of unique identifier assigned to claimants which would generate a pop-up window to identify the claimant when a new claim was submitted. The pop-up would notify the lottery employee that a player profile account already existed. Once a lottery player had been identified as a retail owner or associate, the system would prevent the claim from being processed without being referred to SLED for an investigation. While I wasn't a computer programmer, the suggestion seemed sound to me, and the chief auditor seemed like the best person to correct a flaw in the system.

I told Zavala that in the short time I had been with the lottery I had seen and heard of instances where lottery retail owners and associates only properly identified themselves on their first claim. They then lied on their subsequent claims stating they weren't associated with the lottery so their claim would be processed without an investigation. This meant that the system didn't link their profiles, and only one of the profiles would possibly be flagged. This would provide retail owners, and their associates, with the opportunity to steal a winning lottery ticket from an unsuspecting player. They would receive a payment as long as the ticket was worth less than $250,000. I told Zavala I wasn't great with numbers, but it certainly seemed like a large amount of money was being paid under fraudulent circumstances.

Zavala said this information was interesting but never talked to me again after the presentation. This was the first time I had tried to report a problem to lottery management that I felt needed to be addressed. I expected some sort of action to correct a problem and protect lottery players considering the efforts the lottery had made to show the public how important integrity was. Over time, I would realize that there was no interest in addressing fraud through audits, and the internal auditors were more interested in keeping problems quiet. A year later I would learn that the Lottery Act required an independent audit of the financial statements of the lottery but not of the entire operation itself. The lottery also handles the bids for service and selects the auditing firm based upon the recommendations of Zavala and the internal audits department. There were no external entities serving as checks and balances for the lottery. To my knowledge, there are still none in place today, although some legislation has been introduced to try to fix the lack of checks and balances. This will be discussed in the final chapter.

CHAPTER 8

My Big Move

As much as I enjoyed answering phones and conducting background investigations, I was ready to become a field investigator. The only problem was a major lack of turnover in the lottery at the time, with the exception of retirements. It was a fairly decent retirement job for many retired detectives who were looking to work an additional twenty years so they could receive lifetime medical from the state. This created limited options within the lottery except for headquarters because the senior guys didn't want to be around management. This changed in early 2014 when the investigator who had worked at the Van Nuys, CA, office decided to retire after eighteen years.

Brean knew I was ready to go to the field, so she came to my office to talk. She informed me that the position would be advertised internally, but she didn't expect anyone who had seniority over me to take the transfer because it was one of the busiest offices in the State. I called my girlfriend Natalie and asked her if she wanted to move to Los Angeles. She hated Sacramento and was ready to go, but I was

WHAT ARE THE ODDS?

conflicted.

With the exception of a few years in my early teens, I had spent my life in Sacramento. I had friends and a professional network, and I knew every inch of the city. The thought of moving somewhere that was the complete opposite of everything I knew was terrifying but exciting at the same time. Natalie began applying for jobs and looking for a place to live that afternoon.

A short time later, it was announced statewide that I had gotten the position and would be transferring in two months. I immediately started getting emails from my new lieutenant, Manny Ortiz, and the investigators he supervised welcoming me to the team. My new partner, Jim Jeffra, called me and told me he looked forward to working with me again. We had worked together for a few months at headquarters before he transferred back to Van Nuys because his wife had terrible allergies and couldn't deal with all of the trees. He told me to let him know if he and his wife could do anything to help Natalie and me with our transition to Southern California.

Jeffra was a living legend who had pretty much seen and done it all. He was a Vietnam Veteran, a retired Sheriff's Deputy, a former city council member, and a former member of a school board. He was also interviewed on Dateline after identifying a murder suspect in a cold case while working as a private investigator. Jeffra was one of the nicest and caring people I had ever met. He truly cared about people and would do whatever he could to help someone in need. His sense of humor was sick and twisted, so I knew we were going to get along well. He had also made a lasting impression on me when we previously worked together. He would put instant coffee in his brewed coffee for an "extra kick" as he put it.

Natalie got a job after a few weeks of searching. We began looking for a place to live and lined up several appointments to view apartments. We spent an evening at the Jeffras' home, where we met his wife, Sheri. They were an extremely cute couple who had been together for years. We sat with them and talked for hours, listening to their war stories about life, law enforcement, and marriage.

In a matter of days, we found a place and signed our lease. Natalie and I drove to my new office. The office was quite reminiscent of the beat-down lottery headquarters where I had interviewed a few years earlier. Ortiz, met us at the office to give us a tour. The office was small, overcrowded, and smelled musty. It was my first field office, and it was located behind a Denny's, so I was still excited. The Denny's would eventually serve as a frequent meeting place for Jeffra and me. There was even a post-arrest session there a few months later where I would meet Howie Mandel. The sales staff were welcoming and excited about having me assigned to their office. We returned home and started packing.

Before I left headquarters, I was treated to a going-away luncheon by Brean and Tacchini at the same location where they took retirees. I was thanked for my contributions to the lottery thus far and told that I was leaving with Tacchini's respect and gratitude. While I knew I was making the right decision for my career and sanity, it certainly made it difficult to leave, knowing I had the support of the command staff.

Natalie and I moved to Los Angeles over the course of four long days. We made four trips from Los Angeles to Sacramento to transport vehicles and get things situated. After getting everything moved into our place, we drove the moving truck to the drop-off location in Northridge, CA. I was carrying my off-duty gun in my shorts pocket, which I often did. After dropping off the truck I got in the passenger side of Natalie's little Ford. I leaned back to relax after a long day of moving and met eyes with the passenger in a Los Angeles Police Department (LAPD) cruiser. Apparently, the fact that my girlfriend was driving raised some suspicions because we were being pulled over a few seconds later. I was clearly profiled because my girlfriend was driving, so they probably assumed I had drugs, a gun (which I did), or a warrant.

I was a tourist who was new to the city. I had only watched the LAPD in movies, television shows, and when they were on the news for beating the crap out of someone. I grew up in the hood, and I knew I had a loaded gun in my pocket. I could see the officer in the rearview mirror approaching my side of the car with his hand on his gun. I placed my hands on the dashboard and looked forward, which was what I did when getting pulled over as a passenger in my friend's cars in high school. While the lead officer spoke with Natalie, I identified myself to the other officer and told him I was a peace officer and had a gun in my pocket. He firmly told me to slowly grab my credentials and keep my hands away from my right cargo pocket. Considering I was pretty sure I was going to get shot on my first night as a Los Angeles resident, I did as I was told. The officer took my credentials and told his partner we were good to go. The officer handed back my credentials and said, "Welcome to LA."

CHAPTER 9

Snooky

Driving to the office on my first day was both exciting and aggravating. I lived fifteen miles from the office. We specifically choose the location of our apartment because it was close enough to our jobs that we could take surface streets and avoid freeways. Even so, it took me almost an hour to get to my office. It was the first time I sat in traffic staring at a screen that said it would take me over thirty minutes to get five miles, but it wouldn't be the last. Driving in Los Angeles was different than driving in Sacramento. After a day of driving around Southern California swapping vehicles and meeting people, I returned to the Van Nuys office. Ortiz and Jeffra brought me up to speed on what to expect and showed me the huge region I would be covering.

Ortiz seemed genuine but was also unsure of himself. He was a fairly junior lieutenant who had come from working as a reserve police officer for a local police department. One thing I knew for sure was that he was a yes-man and would need to clear everything with upper management before making a decision.

While we were talking, we were interrupted by one of the front office workers who told me there was a claimant in the lobby claiming the lottery lost her winning ticket. I took the lead because I was the new guy and went to the window to speak with the claimant. She was short and had a striking resemblance to a reality television star, large sunglasses and all. I decided to call her Snooky. I identified myself as an investigator and listened as she told me her story.

Snooky gave me a copy of a Mega Millions ticket with writing all over it containing the names of lottery employees she had spoken to on the phone. She claimed she was the rightful owner of the $324 million prize from last year—the one I had actually assisted with—which was unfortunate for her. She claimed to have made a copy of the ticket before she mailed it to Sacramento and said someone from the lottery lost the ticket.

The copy of the ticket she provided looked as if it had been altered and copied several times. The ticket did contain the winning numbers from the draw, but they were slightly off-center, which made me believe she pasted the numbers from a draw report to the original ticket. Oftentimes, lottery retailers will print what is called a "draw report" that is the size of a regular ticket, which contains the winning numbers from the corresponding draw. It's basically a way for the retailers to be lazy so they don't have to tell customers what the winning numbers were. Snooky forgot to conceal the serial number from her original ticket, which allowed me to research it. I checked the lottery's computer system and located the information for her ticket. The ticket was a loser that had been purchased at a Los Angeles liquor store on the same day the actual winning ticket was sold in San Jose.

Armed with my evidence, I brought Snooky into my office for my first official interrogation.

I asked, "Where did you buy the ticket?"

Snooky replied, "A Liquor Store in LA."

I asked, "When did you buy the ticket."

Snooky replied, "The day it was sold. I know I'm the winner."

I asked, "What did you do with the ticket?"

Snooky replied, "I mailed it to Sacramento. You guys lost it."

I confronted Snooky with the information I had obtained regarding her losing ticket and gave her an opportunity to come clean. I was trying to impress my new boss and partner, so a confession on my first day would be great. She insisted that the information was wrong, and she was the winner. She said she knew the lottery would try to prevent her from getting her money and was going to sue. I brought out the big guns and told her it was a felony to present a forged ticket to the lottery in an effort to claim a prize. She said she had proof of her win in her storage unit and could bring it back to me tomorrow. I told her I would give her a week to come back with her "evidence" or I would arrest her. She never did.

That night, I was invited to go out on an arrest warrant service with my partners from the southern region. Brian Hernandez, Johanna Delgado, and Alvaro Arreola were around the same age as me and loved arresting their own suspects. As lottery investigators, we had the option of filing a case, obtaining an arrest warrant, and referring the arrest to local law enforcement. The problem with referring an arrest to local law enforcement is that they didn't have the time to go out and arrest someone for a lottery crime, and it defeated the purpose of having sworn personnel who can make arrests if you're just going to dump your work on someone else. Lottery investigators were also given take-home cars, which were equipped with lights and sirens. The justification for this was the fact that we would use these state-owned vehicles to engage in peace officer duties outside of simply commuting to and from the office, which was really what most of the investigators did. As a group of new investigators, we felt it was our responsibility to ensure the information being used to justify our take-home cars was factual.

The suspect in question lived in Long Beach, which I only knew from Snoop Dogg songs about the "LBC." It was pretty cool to be riding around in an unmarked cop car wearing a raid vest and looking for a bad guy. The bad guy in question had stolen a decoy scratch-off ticket from one of the investigators during an operation the previous month. The district attorney filed felony charges against the suspect, who had been working as a clerk at a lottery retail location. After several hours of chasing him from house to house, I saw him skateboarding down a busy street. Delgado turned on the lights and siren. We made a U-turn and stopped the car. I got out, yelled "stop," and put him in handcuffs. Because I was 6'1" and fairly stocky, my actions earned me the nickname "Leg Sweep." Hernandez and Arreola were convinced I was going to leg sweep the guy off of his skateboard because of how loud I yelled, so they decided it was an appropriate nickname. Oh, and yes, Al's last name was actually Arreola, so it's not a name I made up to protect someone's identity.

A few weeks later I remembered Snooky was still on my list and looked her up in my system. I was excited to find a no-bail warrant had been issued for her arrest since we had last spoken. This presented the perfect opportunity to arrest her and file charges against her for the false claim while she was in jail. I was able to get her phone number after contacting multiple people she had been couch surfing with. I called her and told her the lottery had found her ticket and was ready to pay her prize. I just needed to get her signature so I could give her a check. Snooky was excited and made an appointment to meet with me the next day.

I got Hernandez, Areola, Delgado, and Jeffra to assist me with my first Los Angeles arrest. Snooky was almost two hours late, but she finally showed up. She was sporting the same big rimmed sunglasses and new hair extensions. My partners and I arrested her and booked her for her warrant and the forged lottery ticket charge. Snooky was convicted and sentenced to serve time in the county jail. This was my first successful case as a field investigator.

CHAPTER 10

Retailer Compliance Program

The Retailer Compliance Program was one of my favorite parts of the job. I was excited to get the opportunity to conduct my first operation at the new office. Jeffra and his former partner hadn't conducted an operation in their region for a while, so I was the undercover operative and lead investigator responsible for all of the paperwork. This was exciting because I was an idiot at the time and didn't realize how much paperwork would be involved. I later realized how smart Jeffra was to capitalize on my youthful excitement because he didn't like writing. We got loaded up and drove to our first location, which was a gas station two blocks away from the Van Nuys office. I decided to use a $20,000 decoy scratch-off ticket since this was my first big operation.

I walked into the gas station and saw a female clerk working behind the counter. After walking around for a few minutes, I placed the ticket on the counter and told her I believed I had won. She took my ticket and checked it on the lottery computer. She told me I wasn't a winner and threw my decoy ticket in the trash can. It was hard to believe the ticket was stolen at our first stop, two blocks away from the office. I got in the car and we drove to the next location while watching the video of the theft because I was still excited.

There are plenty of "real-life" cop stories that talk about the paperwork involved with being a cop and how that part of the job never makes its way into the movies or television. My story is no different because it's all true. Prior to every operation, I had to photocopy the front and back of all of the decoy scratch-off tickets I was using. Every time someone stole a decoy scratch-off ticket, I would download the video footage onto a disc and book it into evidence. The scratch-off ticket had to be flagged as stolen in the lottery system. I would write the first of three reports, which would all be connected to the same case. The other reports were written when the ticket was claimed and when the suspect was arrested. This usually involved three separate interactions with the suspect, provided they didn't flee the country, which happened to Hernandez. I felt bad for the suspect in Hernandez's case because although there was a ton of evidence, and we never lost a decoy scratch-off case, it was still a white-collar crime, which almost always resulted in probation.

The clerk who stole the ticket from me and her fiancé came to the Van Nuys office the next day to claim the stolen scratch-off ticket. Jeff Bermont, the lottery sales manager for Van Nuys, called me right away. He was as excited about the suspect showing up as I was. Bermont believed in what the lottery stood for but also believed clerks who stole tickets from customers should be arrested. He even brought them to the back and took a picture of them holding a big cardboard check while waiting for me to get back.

Ortiz sat in with me when I brought them in to be interviewed because this was my first decoy ticket theft interview. We introduced ourselves to the suspects and congratulated them on their win. The clerk's fiancé actually claimed the ticket. The clerk who stole the ticket came along to share in the excitement. They told us that she was a Muslim and he was a Buddhist, which created a lot of strife between their families. I asked the fiancé how he obtained the ticket he was claiming.

He said, "We were driving back from Vegas and stopped in Primm."

I asked, "The lottery store in Primm?"

He said, "Yes, there. I bought it and scratched it off, but forgot about it."

I said, "So, you bought the ticket and scratched it off?"

He said, "Yes, and saw all the zeros."

After locking him into his bogus story about how he had bought the ticket, I broke the news to them about the ticket being a decoy. I asked the clerk who stole the ticket if she recognized me. She said she did not. I told her I was undercover at the business and had given her the ticket to check. She admitted to taking the ticket, saying she believed it was "A gift from God." I told her it wasn't a gift from God but the devil because she had stolen it from the person it actually belonged to. She said she took the ticket and brought it to her fiancé when she got off work. The clerk's fiancé also worked at a lottery retail location a few blocks away. They checked the ticket again to see how much it was worth, then concocted a plan to claim the money and decided he would claim it.

I had no idea what I was doing when I took the case to the district attorney in Van Nuys because none of the current investigators, or Ortiz, had filed a case there. I used the search engine on my phone to find the Van Nuys Courthouse. After going to three different buildings, I finally found the district attorney's office. The secretary was nice enough to walk me through the process and not make me feel like an idiot for not knowing what I needed to do. This involved multiple forms I hadn't filled out and signing in. I was told that the priority was given to the most serious crimes, which my scratch-off ticket theft was not. I waited for an LAPD homicide and robbery detective to go back to meet with the district attorney before I was finally called.

The filing district attorney who met with me was a salty old guy who had been with the County for over thirty years. I was sure he was going to give me crap when I told him why I was there, but I was pleasantly surprised. He didn't know the lottery had a police department and had never filed a case from a lottery investigator. He was excited and treated me like I was a rock star, even calling in other attorneys to show me off like I was a shiny new car. He read my case and complimented me on being so thorough. I always conducted investigations in a fair manner, documenting all of the facts, even if they hurt my case. This style was not always well-received, but my cases were rarely challenged in court because most defense attorneys would opt to take a plea bargain for their clients.

The district attorney filed several felony charges against my suspects, which resulted in a warrant for their arrest. My partners and I arrested them and transported them to jail. Both suspects took a plea bargain for probation. They were both prohibited from working at a lottery retail location during the length of their probation, which was a common condition I was able to obtain when dealing with suspects who committed crimes against lottery customers, even when those customers were undercover investigators. There were no lottery regulations that prohibited an employee with a criminal record from working in a lottery retail location, though—even if the employee specifically victimized a lottery customer. The lottery didn't keep records of these individuals and had no interest in changing regulations to require background investigations or a criminal history check for lottery retail employees. Keeping these individuals from preying on unsuspecting winners was the least I could do.

I conducted numerous Retailer Compliance Program operations in my region while working as a lottery investigator. My decoy scratch-off tickets continued being stolen despite multiple arrests, convictions, word of mouth, and coverage in the local news. Usually, three to four clerks would steal the decoy ticket from my partners and me during each operation. The cases were filed with little to no difficulty because of the nature of the theft. District attorneys in multiple counties were disgusted that a clerk would prey upon the hopes and dreams of lottery customers by stealing a winning ticket. The suspects in my cases were lottery retail owners, their employees, family members, spouses, and acquaintances.

You never knew who would steal a ticket while conducting Retailer Compliance Programs. I had just as many decoy tickets stolen at retail locations that were dumps as I did from ones that looked beautiful. This occurred in high-end communities and poor communities. Sometimes, the clerk would give me a few bucks after telling me my ticket was a low-value winner, but most of the time, they told me the ticket wasn't a winner and kept it. Some stores were placed on lottery probation after an employee stole a decoy ticket and would get a second violation when a ticket was stolen by a different employee. I didn't have a single location's lottery contract pulled after a second violation regardless of how egregious it was because lottery management wouldn't allow it.

There was never enough time to conduct the number of operations in my region as I wanted because of the high volume of cases. Some regions never conducted operations at all. Jeffra suggested putting together a task force that would specialize in conducting Retailer Compliance Programs statewide. His suggestion was ignored.

The number of operations drastically declined during my last year with the lottery. While LaBrie used the Retailer Compliance Program as one of the major selling points when the lottery obtained its level four certification from the World Lottery Association, there wasn't a big push to continue conducting operations. Leadership also micromanaged and put restrictions on investigators that made them so robotic that there was no way a clerk wouldn't know it was an undercover cop handing them a ticket. It was certainly the end of an era to see something that made me want to work for the lottery become such a shell of what it was. Nothing good lasts forever.

CHAPTER 11

Calabasas Oil

I apologize in advance, but in order to understand how scratch-off ticket embezzlement cases work, I have to explain the lottery computer systems and how they work. Embezzlement cases were a crucial part of the whistleblower complaint we would eventually file. Lottery scratch-off tickets are a retail item similar to alcohol and soda. The tickets are paid for by the lottery and are manufactured by an outside company. The tickets are packaged as part of a scratch-off ticket pack and are individually priced for retail sale. The retail price of each scratch-off ticket varies, depending on the game. Scratch-off tickets are distributed to retail locations throughout the state by the lottery from one of two distribution warehouses.

The number of scratch-off ticket packs received by an individual lottery retail location depends on the volume of sales for the location and the orders placed by the lottery sales representative. Each lottery retail location is assigned a letter grade based on their sales numbers from "A" to "D." This means that lottery retail locations could have hundreds or thousands of scratch-off tickets in their possession at any given time.

When a lottery retail location receives a pack of scratch-off tickets, they are considered "confirmed" by the retail location, but they aren't active for sale. A scratch-off ticket still holds retail value but is just a piece of paper worth the cost of manufacturing until the retail location activates the pack to be sold. The cash prize for a winning ticket cannot be paid until the scratch-off ticket pack it came from is activated for sale. The retail location is billed for the retail value of the scratch-off tickets in their possession when the pack "settles." A pack of scratch-off tickets settles when 80% of the winning tickets worth less than $599 are paid out or fifty days since the pack was activated for sale have passed, whichever comes first.

The incentive for a business owner to sell lottery products comes in the form of commissions and reimbursements. Not to mention the fact that a customer will usually purchase alcohol, cigarettes, food, and other items along with their lottery ticket. This is why some of the top-selling locations in California are smoke shops. Retail owners receive a commission on all of the lottery tickets they sell and are reimbursed for all of the scratch-off tickets they don't sell if they return them to the lottery. A retail owner is reimbursed for all of the winning tickets paid out to customers at their location.

In most cases, the lottery will reimburse a retail owner for stolen scratch-off tickets as long as they meet certain requirements, such as notifying the lottery of the theft within four hours and maintaining an inventory of the tickets in their possession. While the lottery has the ability to track all of the scratch-off ticket packs assigned to a retail location and the location where the tickets are validated as a winner or a loser, they don't track each individual ticket sale. As previously discussed, such a system could be implemented, but there was no attempt to do so while I was an employee despite the issue being raised by investigators multiple times.

The lottery won't reimburse lottery retail owners for scratch-off tickets that are embezzled by one of their employees. The majority of retail owners don't realize this when they sign their contract, even though it's clearly stated. Like most of us when reviewing the contract for our cell phone provider, most lottery retailers fail to read all of the fine print. Being the one who had to explain this technicality to a victim was always stressful because the owner realized in that moment they were on the hook for the loss, which was usually quite substantial. There were times when I was screamed at, cussed out, and had to listen to the owner of a business cry because they realized they would end up being bankrupt.

The victims of scratch-off ticket embezzlements were often individuals who owned multiple locations and didn't track their inventory because the books always seemed to balance out in the form of commissions. After a few months of the books not balancing, it was usually their accountant who would realize something was seriously wrong and tell the owner, who would then call the lottery. The extended timeframe allowed the suspect to steal thousands in scratch-off tickets from their employer and thousands more from the state by receiving the cash prize for the stolen tickets.

Shortly after starting at the Van Nuys office, I was assigned my first embezzlement case. The case involved an employee who was stealing entire packs of scratch-off tickets from the gas station where he was working in Calabasas. The owner came to my office with a large black trash bag. We sat down and discussed what had been occurring at his business. He told me the suspect employee had been identified and admitted to stealing "a few" packs of tickets. The employee brought the bag to work and gave it to the owner. The employee then confessed to the theft on cell phone video and indicated he had been working with an accomplice.

The owner and the suspect employee were both Egyptian, so the owner was originally going to handle the theft himself because he knew the family of the suspect. Initially, the suspect's family had agreed to pay back the loss to the owner. When the owner and his manager realized that the loss was over $30,000, they decided to pursue criminal charges. The owner gave me copies of the store's surveillance system which contained footage from several shifts when the suspect employee was working. The footage showed the employee placing 2–6 packs of scratch-off tickets on the counter at least once per shift. Each time, he activated the packs for sale using the store's lottery computer.

When the thefts originally started, the suspect employee would hand the packs to his accomplice at the counter. The accomplice would stand in the store for hours scratching tickets and checking them on the self-check terminal while the employee helped customers. The accomplice would check the tickets while they were still attached to the roll, and would only tear off the winners. He then handed the winning tickets to the employee, who would open the register and remove the cash. The accomplice took the cash from the employee and left the store.

This continued on several occasions until the two of them realized the store surveillance cameras were recording their actions. When the accomplice stopped coming into the business, the employee would activate the ticket packs and place them on the counter. He positioned himself so the tickets were in front of him, and his back was to the camera. He placed the scratch-off tickets in his waistband, zipped up his jacket, and exited the store. The employee would meet with his accomplice in the parking lot, where the accomplice was sitting in a parked car. Because these two were so "smart," the employee would open the rear passenger door and place the tickets on the seat. The employee would close the door and head back inside. The accomplice would leave the parking lot and find a place to scratch off the tickets.

The accomplice was extremely easy to identify because he was short, skinny, and wore multiple gold chains. He was also nice enough to wear the same ridiculous hat which had gigantic gold letters on the front everywhere he went. As you already know, all scratch-off tickets can be tracked. I began running reports to find patterns and quickly located all of the stolen packs. The packs I had received from the owner were a small percentage of what the suspects actually stole. I began driving to the different lottery retail stores where the stolen tickets had been paid out. Every surveillance system showed the accomplice entering the business wearing the gold chains and ugly hat. He frequently handed the clerk a stack of scratch-off tickets to cash out. He was always generous and gave the clerk a tip in the form of cash, or scratch-off tickets. I would later discover the accomplice worked for a lottery retailer and knew how the system worked.

One thing that bothered me was the fact that the lottery had high-tech systems but didn't notice such a blatant pattern of theft. The sales at this particular store began going up at a noticeable rate for no reason. I knew the lottery had the ability to notify SLED when a retail location sold a certain amount of online tickets, but I didn't understand why the same concept wasn't applied to scratch-off tickets. After all, the notification system would be easy to implement. Lottery retail locations are billed weekly for the scratch-off tickets they sell. The bill is itemized and available for review by lottery employees who have access to the system. Since a retail location is graded, the lottery has an idea of what a typical bill should be. The system could easily be programmed to alert SLED, or another division within the lottery when there is a significant increase in the bill.

I mentioned this idea to Jeffra, thinking I was a genius and could save the lottery and the state money. Jeffra told me he and several investigators had already made this suggestion to lottery management multiple times. They were told that a change to the system could cause delays and impact sales. Jeffra had worked a case the previous year involving two lottery retail owners who were playing their scratch-off ticket inventory without paying for it. The retail owners were husband and wife. The wife was addicted to gambling and was highly intelligent.

The husband and wife knew how their store was billed by the lottery and began playing the scratch-off tickets without paying for them. They would scratch off the entire pack and cash out 79% of the winning tickets to avoid being billed. The store's grade improved, which meant the sales representative's commission was increasing. The sales representative helped to facilitate the ordering of new tickets, and the warehouse kept sending them.

After a few months, the store started having "Non-Sufficient

Funds (NSF)" when the lottery attempted to bill it for scratch-off tickets. The wife would send in winning tickets worth $600 or more to the lottery and would use the winnings to make payments toward the NSF. Despite the NSF, the lottery continued sending tickets to the business, which the owners continued to play without paying for. The lottery's revenue collections wouldn't place a hold on the account to stop it from receiving new tickets and wouldn't contact the warehouse to stop shipments to the store. This continued until the lottery finally involved SLED and assigned the case to Jeffra.

Due to the lack of accountability, the total loss to the lottery was over $125,000. The case didn't sit well with Jeffra even though he was able to file charges against the owners with the district attorney. He realized that the owners had a serious gambling addiction and believed the lottery failed to recognize the issue and intervene, even though there were multiple red flags. He voiced his concerns and the need for a red flag notification system to deputy directors and his lieutenant. No action was taken, and similar cases continued to occur. (Jeffra J. , 2013)

I contacted Ortiz because I saw some similarities between Jeffra's case and mine. I explained how this loss was preventable and suggested the implementation of a notification system. Ortiz said he would relay the suggestion to his superiors and never gave me an update. Jeffra and I would bring this issue to lottery management several times with no response. The system was never implemented, and large-scale losses have continued to occur to this day.

Jeffra told me the flaws in the system were so bad, one retailer had closed his shop and kept the lottery equipment that had been assigned to him. He changed his business address to his personal residence and the lottery failed to check to see if the address was business or residential. He continued to have scratch-off tickets sent to his home address, where he would scratch off the tickets and collect the winnings. This continued until his actions were discovered by the retired investigator from the Van Nuys office.

I returned to my investigation and tried to serve the victim. I interviewed the accomplice who admitted to his role in the crime but insisted the employee was the mastermind. He told me he was an Egyptian rapper who was up-and-coming in the underground rap scene. The crime was orchestrated by the employee as a way to pay the Egyptian rapper back for gold chains he had given him which were worth thousands. He told me about multiple trips to Egypt where he purchased multiple chains, which he would give away like candy. He even offered me a necklace, but I told him I didn't look good wearing gold.

I tried to talk to the employee, but his family was wealthy and refused to let him talk to me. I took the case to the district attorney for filing. I was assigned to the most difficult lawyer I had ever met. He met with me for almost five hours over the course of two days before finally filing charges against both suspects. I obtained an arrest warrant for the employee and Egyptian rapper and assembled an arrest team. The Egyptian rapper was a frequent flyer at the jail, having been arrested several times. He wasn't surprised when we showed up at his house and took him into custody. He was one of the funniest guys I have ever arrested because he kept begging Hernandez to turn on the lights and siren while we were driving him to the jail. He kept calling Hernandez "Paul Walker" because he was "Fast and Furious," which made the rest of us laugh.

Word quickly got out that we had arrested the Egyptian rapper. While booking him into jail I received a call from a lawyer who told me he represented the family of the employee. He gave me a list of demands on how his client would be arrested and refused to allow him to be booked into the main jail. We made arrangements for the suspect employee to surrender himself at the West Hollywood sheriff's station, even though I believed he needed to go to grown-up jail.

The employee and his mother arrived at the jail an hour and a half late. She told me her son was not to be placed in handcuffs, and a bail bondsman was on the way so he wouldn't be in jail for too long. I placed him in handcuffs anyway and walked him over to Hernandez's car. After placing him in the back seat, we drove around to the back of the station. I walked the halls of the sheriff's station and couldn't find a supervisor anywhere, so I was left with no choice but to take him to grown-up jail, which didn't upset me.

The employee turned pale as we pulled into the sally port of the main jail in downtown Los Angeles. We booked him and began the long walk past the large windows of the holding cell where recently bused-in inmates from the sheriff's sub stations were seated. Hernandez and I looked at the inmates sitting against the wall and saw the Egyptian rapper. He smiled and waved to us as if we were all good friends, which gave Hernandez and me a great laugh.

While I couldn't guarantee the victim in the case would receive a penny from the suspects to offset his loss, I felt taking them to jail was the least I could do. The court system always works out a deal for offenders, which results in a small amount of time actually being spent in jail, especially when you can hire an expensive attorney. This never sits well with victims, which I completely understand. Because of this, I always made it a point to let them know that the lottery had done its part to work for them and ensure the suspects were brought to justice. In a way, this made me feel better, considering the lottery could have prevented the loss in the first place but chose not to. (Galbreath, 14-1121, 2014)

Lottery investigators continued having embezzlement cases assigned to them until the day I left. Jeffra and I handled too many to count in our office alone. The cases were always similar and could have been prevented. In most of the cases, the lottery sales representative noticed an unexplained spike in scratch-off ticket sales for a location and notified their supervisor in the form of an online message. The supervisor wouldn't notify SLED of a suspicious sales spike, and the sales representative would take no further action because they received a commission for the sales in their assigned region. I still don't understand how the State of California would allow a public employee to make a salary that includes commissions and bonuses.

CHAPTER 12

Discounting

Lottery retail locations are only allowed to pay prizes of $599 or less. It is a violation of their contract and lottery regulations to purchase a winning ticket from a winner for less than the actual prize value. These regulations are clearly stated in the sales contract they sign with the lottery. When a lottery retail owner, or associate, purchases a winning ticket from a winner for a fraction of the prize value, it is called "discounting." This is simply a phrase used by the lottery to downplay a blatant felony act to avoid criminally prosecuting retail owners.

David Goldstein, a reporter from CBS2 in Los Angeles, did an investigative report on the disproportionate number of winners who are lottery retail owners. Goldstein even included a mathematician who shared statistics on the unbelievable win rates from the lottery retailers, their family members, and friends. Goldstein interviewed Tacchini about some of the retail owners. During the interview, Goldstein asked Tacchini about one particular retailer who had won three out of four times at his business. Tacchini said, "he may be purchasing tickets from customers, which is a violation of our regulations. We know that does occur." This statement wasn't accurate because discounting is not only a violation of regulations, but it can also be a crime. Tacchini's response was a carefully crafted response, but in all fairness, Corporate Communications were heavily involved in all media interviews. Whenever I saw Tacchini being interviewed as the deputy director of SLED, a Corporate Communications representative was visible in the background. The lottery tells the news media discounting isn't a crime, which may be accurate if we are only examining the act of purchasing the winning ticket from a customer. The act of claiming the purchased ticket is a crime. The report ended with a cop-out statement from the lottery who said, "Without absolute proof, it's difficult to break the contracts with retailers. In fact, they've been sued for doing so in the past. This story was the first time I had seen the lottery mention past lawsuits as a reason for not terminating lottery contracts. (Goldstein, CBS Los Angeles, 2014)

After discounting a winning ticket, a lottery retailer has to submit a lottery claim form in order to claim the cash prize. On that form, the lottery retailer signs under penalty of perjury, which is also a crime, stating they are the rightful owner of the ticket they are claiming. I will get into the specific definition of a lottery ticket "winner" in chapter 16. (California, 2021)

Prizes claimed with the lottery are issued in the form of a signed check or pay warrant from the state controller. The state controller's office will run winners for financial obligations such as child support, alimony, victim restitution, back taxes, and other liens. This means money won by an individual who owes money to a child or other entitled person or entity won't see their money. Instead, the money is redirected to the rightful recipient. Being a child who was raised in poverty with no child support from one of their parents, I was a supporter of an individual paying their debts if they were lucky enough to win.

Someone who knows they owe money to a spouse, back taxes, liens, etc., will often offer to sell their winning ticket at a discounted price to a retail owner, employee, relative, friend, or stranger. If a claim is investigated, and it is determined the ticket was discounted, the claim is to be denied according to lottery regulations. This type of activity isn't necessarily criminal due to the fact that the purchaser may not realize they aren't allowed to purchase a winning ticket from another party. The denied claim becomes a part of the unclaimed prize pool, which is automatically given to public schools at the end of the year.

Discounting becomes criminal when a retail owner or their employee deceives a winner with misinformation in order to profit from the deception. This often involves individuals who are not United States citizens. SLED investigated numerous cases where retail owners asked winners if they are United States citizens, and if the winner told them they were not, the retail owner told them they cannot claim their prize because of their citizenship status. The retail owner would then offer the winner a fraction of what their prize is worth because it was better than receiving nothing. The retail owner profits from the purchase because of the difference between what the ticket was actually worth and what they paid the winner. The majority of these victims are Hispanic because of the fear of reporting thefts to the government out of fear of deportation. One major problem with this is the fact that the lottery targets Hispanic players with predatory advertising in the form of billboards, radio ads, and Hispanic-themed lottery games.

As discussed earlier, the lottery's own research showed the majority of their customer base was located in the poorest communities. The lottery even awards contracts to companies that specialize in advertising to the Hispanic community. I have personally witnessed lottery retail locations that have dozens of Hispanic players sitting inside and outside of the business scratching multiple tickets. The winners go right back inside and purchase more tickets with the winnings from the tickets they have already purchased. You won't find problem-gambling brochures inside of these locations, nor will you have a lottery representative approaching these individuals and offering them help for potential gambling addiction. These players are the driving force behind the profits for the lottery. The money they spend allows the deputy director of the lottery to send out emails that brag about sales numbers and increase sales projections for the coming year. (Johnson, Item 9(a) – Hispanic Market Advertising Services Contract, 2019)

It would be reasonable to expect the lottery to take steps to prosecute retail owners who prey on the most venerable and terminate their contracts to protect the public. Instead, the lottery calls all forms of winning ticket purchasing "discounting," even when it's criminal. Every fraudulent discounting case is a felony. These cases would be easily prosecutable, but I didn't see a single prosecution for discounting while I was employed by the lottery, even after trying to prosecute a few myself. Retail owners who discounted winning tickets didn't have their contract terminated; instead, they were offered voluntary retailer probation. In most instances, they would still keep their contract when they were caught doing it again; they would just have their probation period extended. The lottery didn't like terminating retailer contracts, even when it was warranted or should have been required.

My first discounting case has stuck with me to this day. I was assigned a retailer submitted a claim because the ticket he submitted wasn't purchased from the lottery retail location he owned. The ticket was checked at several different retail locations before it was checked at the store he owned. This type of ticket validation activity was suspicious, indicating the ticket was "shopped around" by the winner before it was discounted. Jeffra and I drove out to the retail location, which was in Ventura, CA. I always loved driving to Ventura because the view and the weather, was usually beautiful.

The business was a small gas station located off the freeway that had a convenience store inside. The owner was working behind the counter when we walked inside. He was arrogant and dismissive when I identified myself as a lottery investigator. I told him I was investigating the claim he had submitted and showed him a picture of the ticket he had claimed. After initially telling me he purchased the ticket, and scratched off the play area, he admitted to discounting. He said he purchased the ticket from a female employee of his business who wasn't a citizen. She worked under the table at several different employers, including his.

The owner stated he often did her favors by giving her cash advances on her paycheck to help her out since she was a single mother. He gave her a few hundred dollars for the ticket. He claimed the cash prize because she owed him money anyway, so this allowed her to repay her debt. He said he also knew she couldn't claim the ticket because she was not a citizen, so he was doing her a favor. The owner was pissed when I told him he wasn't getting paid. I told him his employee would need to contact me so she could claim her prize since she was the rightful owner.

A few weeks later, the employee contacted me and scheduled an interview. After reassuring her that she wasn't in any trouble, I asked her to tell me about the ticket. She told me where and when she had purchased the ticket. She even knew where she had taken the ticket to check it. She ultimately took the ticket to her boss because she wasn't sure what to do, having never won a large prize. Her boss told her she had to be a citizen to claim the prize, so she agreed to receive a small amount of cash for the ticket.

She told me she really needed the money because she wasn't a United States citizen and was raising three children on her own. Her husband had left her for another woman and wasn't providing her any money to help take care of their children. She worked in the fields and did other odd jobs to pay her bills and take care of her family. She began sobbing as she told me she often had to take loans from her boss at the gas station to survive. I had her fill out a claim form and explained to her how the lottery worked with the hope she would one day claim a large prize again. She never did.

The owner of the gas station was victimizing his employee. I suspected he had victimized others based on his past claims, but I had no proof. I recommended his contract be terminated for the violation and recommended pursuing criminal charges based upon the fact he had committed perjury. My recommendations were ignored and he was offered retailer probation. He is still selling lottery products to this day. (Galbreath, Unknown Report Number, 2014)

My next discounting case involved a lottery retail owner in Panorama City. He had multiple claims on file with the lottery and had claimed a scratch-off ticket that appeared to have been shopped around before it was brought to his store. I interviewed him at my office and explained the reason for his claim being investigated. Much to my surprise, he said he didn't buy the ticket and wanted to tell me the truth. He told me he had purchased the ticket from a former employee who didn't want to claim it because he owed child support. He said several lottery retail owners know who he is and buy winning tickets from him all the time.

I asked the owner for the winner's name and the locations that were discounting. The owner told me he wasn't a snitch and refused to give me any other information. I denied his claim and recommended termination of his contract. My recommendation was ignored. (Galbreath, Unknown Report Number, 2014)

The last discounting case I will discuss in this book involved a donut shop owner in Panorama City. I was assigned a claim for a winning scratch-off ticket which was submitted by a retail owner. In researching the ticket submitted by the retail owner, I discovered that the ticket had been assigned to a different retail location a few blocks away and was checked at different locations prior to being checked at the donut shop. The ticket had all of the indicators of being shopped around prior to it being claimed with the lottery. The ticket was worth $1,000.

I responded to the donut shop and interviewed the owner. He initially told me he had purchased the ticket from his own store, scratched off the play area, and discovered he was a winner. I confronted the owner with the fact that the ticket hadn't been sold at his shop and had been checked at several locations prior to being checked at his shop. The owner admitted he had purchased the ticket from an undocumented immigrant who was his good friend. I asked him for his friend's name and contact information, which he couldn't provide me. I asked him how much he had paid his "friend" and he told me he had paid him $750. I gave the owner my business card and asked him to have the rightful owner of the ticket contact me should he return to the store. He never contacted me.

I suspected that the owner was knowingly targeting undocumented immigrants and providing them with false information, but I couldn't prove it. I was frustrated about having to investigate this business again because I had raided it with the LAPD about a year earlier for operating an illegal casino, which included rigged slot machines. The shop had two large televisions which were always on a Spanish language channel, sold Mexican pastries, international calling cards, and was frequently packed with Hispanic males. The owner and his wife ran the shop mostly themselves.

The shop was raided following a tip that they were bringing the slot machines out at night. According to the tipster, two of their family members had gambling addictions, which resulted in them spending their entire paychecks on the slot machines. Prior to the raid, I went into the shop undercover and played the machine myself. When I returned with LAPD, we found another machine in the back. On this particular night, there was an employee who wasn't related to the owners working the front counter. She told me that if I had come in a week earlier, I would have found the third machine in operation, which actually dispensed cash when you won. In my report, I recommended filing criminal charges against the owners and terminating their lottery contract. My recommendations were ignored, and the owner was placed on retailer probation.

Jeffra told me he had also investigated the owner a year earlier for lying on his claim form by stating he wasn't a lottery retail owner. The owner had stated he was tired while filling out the form and had simply made a mistake. I was now investigating him a year later for yet again failing to disclose his lottery retail ownership and had previously investigated the illegal gaming operation. There was an obvious criminal pattern with the business.

I began researching the owner's previous claims. I believed this new development, coupled with all of the past issues, might result in some sort of action from the lottery based on my investigation. The retailer owner had claimed over fifteen winning scratch-off tickets for several thousand dollars. He checked the "no" box when asked if he owned a lottery retail location, worked at a lottery retail location, or was related to a lottery retail owner. I now had evidence that the owner had committed perjury on several occasions.

While conducting my research I was approached by the sales associate who was assigned to the donut shop. He informed me that a guy had approached him and told him that the owner bought a scratch-off ticket from him which was worth $25,000. The owner asked the guy if he was a US citizen. When he told the owner he was undocumented, the owner told him he couldn't claim the ticket. The owner offered to pay the unsuspecting victim $15,000 for the winning ticket and never informed him he could claim the ticket on his own. The individual felt that he had been victimized and knew of other undocumented individuals who had also been victimized but didn't want to come forward because of their citizenship status. He wanted the sales associate to know so it wouldn't happen to someone else. I researched the claim history of the male owner and his wife. I found the $25,000 ticket and discovered it had been paid to his wife. I was still hard-pressed to pursue criminal charges because the victim would not come forward and the owner had checked the appropriate boxes on this claim.

The next day, I went to the district attorney's office to file a case. I was assigned the district attorney who had handled my first case, and I took the opportunity to discuss the donut shop owner. I explained the "discounting" case I couldn't prove, my past experiences with the location, and the abundance of perjury committed by the owner. While I couldn't get justice for the victim in the $25,000 case, I could at least send the message that there were checks and balances by charging him with perjury for the tickets he had claimed. The district attorney told me he would be more than happy to sign off on my case if I brought it back to him.

I completed my report and contacted Ortiz to inform him of my recommendations. Ortiz was very apprehensive about arresting a retailer for committing perjury related to discounting. Ortiz said he would run it by management and get back to me. Instead, Ortiz did nothing and let my report sit in his queue in the lottery report writing system. The report would sit there for almost a year, but we'll get to that later. (Galbreath, 15-2615, 2015)

CHAPTER 13

Donut Queen

In mid-2014, a concerned customer contacted Bermont. The customer said he had purchased a scratch-off ticket from a donut shop in Simi Valley. He looked at the ticket and noticed a small portion of the play area had been removed. He knew the exposed area was the location where the "Void if removed number (VIRN)" was located. He brought the issue to the attention of the clerk. She was dismissive but gave him another ticket from under the counter. That ticket was also altered, so he took it and left the store. He scratched off the play area and had been sold a losing ticket. The customer believed the clerk knew the ticket was a loser when she sold it to him.

The incident the player described was a common problem for the lottery called "pinning." All scratch-off lottery tickets had a VIRN which was located on the bottom of the ticket under the scratch-off laminate. In order to validate a scratch-off ticket as a winner or a loser, the clerk would need to scan the back of the ticket and enter three numbers from the VIRN into the computer. The designated numbers were contained inside of a box and were always different. This was an added layer of protection to prevent lottery retail clerks from identifying the winning tickets from a pack.

Pinning occurred when a suspect used an object, such as a safety pin, to remove a small amount of the scratch-off laminate which concealed the VIRN. The suspect would scan the barcode on the back of the ticket and attempt to guess the VIRN based on the portions of the numbers they could see. Every incorrect guess was recorded in the lottery's computer system, but no notification system was implemented to notify SLED when a VIRN was incorrectly guessed multiple times. Pinning always provided a large amount of evidence but resulted in a district attorney asking why the lottery didn't know it was occurring.

The lottery didn't consider pinning to be a major problem when I began investigating the customer's complaint. I called him and obtained a statement. He gave me the ticket information and the date he'd purchased it. I reviewed the history for the ticket and discovered the VIRN was entered incorrectly several times a few days before he purchased it. The ticket was, in fact, a loser, and most of the pack appeared to have been pinned as well based on the VIRN from almost every ticket being entered incorrectly several times.

Armed with my evidence, I decided to drive to the donut shop. I really had no idea what the hell I was doing because neither Ortiz nor Jeffra had ever had a pinning case. Although the lottery had investigated multiple pinning cases over the years, there was never an official training put together to show how the case should be investigated. I decided to enter the business and act like a dumb lottery cop, which I was, who was just stopping in to conduct a random inspection. Lottery retail owners agree to allow lottery employees access to their business to conduct an inspection at any time during normal business hours. If I saw something that looked suspicious, I would simply play stupid and act like I didn't know what I was looking at.

When I walked in, I saw one female employee working inside of the business and one customer at the counter. After she finished helping the customer, I approached her and identified myself. I told her the lottery believed the location may be selling damaged tickets, so I was doing an inspection to clear things up. She was happy to help and invited me behind the counter. I immediately noticed several tickets sitting under the counter which had been torn off of their ticket packs. The packs the tickets had been torn from were still inside of the plastic display. Separating individual tickets from the pack isn't something the average Lottery ticket seller does. Occasionally, a customer will change their mind while purchasing scratch-off tickets, but I had never seen this many.

I told the clerk I believed I had found the problem tickets. I took five of the tickets from under the counter and inspected them. I noticed a small scratch in the laminate where the VIRN is located on each of the tickets. I took pictures of the tickets so I could check them later. I thanked the clerk and told her the issue had been resolved. She offered me a donut as I left for the inconvenience, which I denied because I refused to live the stereotype, but the donuts did look good.

I drove a few blocks away and parked. I called Ortiz and told him what I saw. He told me I should go back to the store and confiscate all of their lottery inventory. I told him I believed we could obtain enough evidence to get a search warrant for the donut shop and the owner's residence. After a mild argument about rules of evidence, and my insistence that we consult with the Ventura County district attorney, Ortiz agreed to let me get the opinion of the district attorney before proceeding.

I returned to my office and checked the tickets I had photographed. All of the tickets had been checked prior to my visit, and all of them were losing tickets. The VIRN for each ticket had been guessed incorrectly multiple times before being identified as a loser. I knew I was in over my head on this case and would get little assistance from Ortiz, so I contacted Tristant. He was the resident expert on the lottery's computer systems and knew what reports to run and how to identify pinning activity. He walked me through running an embezzlement report on the retail location, which shows suspicious validation activity on the terminal during specific timeframes at the location. Validation activity is the technical term for checking tickets to see if they were a winner or a loser on the lottery computer terminal.

I ran the report for a period of one week and found multiple instances of pinning on just about every scratch-off ticket assigned to the business. I located the most recently pinned tickets and created a list for an undercover buy. Jeffra agreed to go to the donut shop undercover, posing as a confused elderly customer. After initially telling me to "fornicate" myself for calling him old, he agreed to help. Jeffra purchased three tickets from the same clerk who had been working during my previous visit. He played up the confused old man card, which she capitalized on by selling him several losing tickets from under the counter. After returning to my office, I checked the tickets he had purchased to confirm my suspicions. All of the tickets had been pinned and identified as losing tickets days before being sold to Jeffra.

I contacted the Ventura County district attorney's office and was put in touch with a special prosecutor who specialized in consumer protection. She and her lead investigator were excited to prosecute such a unique case and were amazed to discover the lottery had investigators. Jeffra, one of my other partners, and I met with the special prosecutor and her lead Investigator the next day at a coffee shop. I presented the evidence I had already obtained and told them about the initial victim. The special prosecutor agreed with my desire for a warrant and offered to provide a surveillance team to establish residency for the owner and associates.

They joined us for another successful undercover purchase of pinned scratch-off tickets. The same clerk was working behind the counter. This time, the clerk sold tickets, which had all been identified as losing tickets prior to the purchase, to the Special Prosecutor and her Lead Investigator. After reviewing previous claims for winning tickets, I was able to identify the clerk, the owner, and the owner's wife. The clerk was the sister-in-law of the owner and worked at the business almost every day. I received a report from the surveillance team which confirmed the residency of the owner. The sister-in-law lived with the owner. She attended community college in the evenings and started early at the donut shop. None of them had criminal records, so they wouldn't have been on anyone's radar had the concerned customer not reported their suspicions.

After obtaining the name of the owner's wife, I found prior claims she had filed with the lottery. She had been paid several thousand dollars from pinned tickets. She didn't identify herself as a lottery retail owner on any of her claim forms, and none of her claims had been assigned to the field for further investigation. The validation reports for the tickets she had claimed showed extensive pinning activity. The claims were filed over a one-year period, which meant it was another missed opportunity by the lottery to protect its customers by establishing safeguards.

I obtained a search warrant for the donut shop and the private residence of the owner. The special prosecutor assembled a team of local law enforcement to assist with a simultaneous search warrant service. There was a sense of shock when my partners and I arrived at the designated meeting location. There were eight of us and thirty of them. We were part of a team of almost forty peace officers representing six different agencies from Ventura County. This was one of my proudest moments because it was my case that made it happen. The special prosecutor commended my work in front of the warrant service team, which included Ortiz. I was happy he was there to hear it, considering he had tried to kill my investigation in the early stages.

We separated into two teams. One would hit the donut shop while the other hit the residence. I was made the team leader for the donut shop, which meant I would get to live the secret dream of every cop. I was about to raid a donut shop. We approached the location with guns drawn. This was probably quite the sight for any onlookers passing by during the early morning commute. As we entered the shop, one of the sheriff's deputies secured the elderly customers who were sitting at one of the tables scratching off lottery tickets. We arrested the sister-in-law, detained the owner, and photographed the business before we started our search. We located a shoulder bag that contained a few thousand scratch-off tickets, which had been pinned. We found additional pinned tickets in the dispenser and scattered throughout the business.

I read the sister in law her Miranda Rights and asked her if she wanted to talk to me about what was occurring at the business. She surprisingly agreed to talk to me. We sat in one of the booths in the lobby of the shop. She told me the entire thing was her idea and that her family had no idea what was happening. I explained to her how the process worked and told her that I believed her family was involved, particularly her brother-in-law. Her face grew pale, and she started shaking. It appeared she was terrified of her brother-in-law. She insisted the entire thing was her own doing and refused to give me any information on the owner.

I brought the owner back into the shop and treated him like a victim, although I believed he was lying. He acted shocked and told me how disappointed he was in his sister-in-law. I asked him if he had any idea what she had been doing. He insisted he knew nothing and had no clue there were any issues with the lottery. He was just concerned about how this was going to make his business and family look.

Prior to arriving at the business, we received permission from the lottery executive staff to suspend the lottery contract at the Donut Queen, which was an absolute surprise for me considering their track record of giving probation to problematic retail owners. Lottery representatives began taking everything not related to the case as evidence, including the lottery signs hanging in the windows. One of them eventually made its way to the wall in my office. The sales representative showed up while we were still securing lottery property. He was sweating and seemed to be nervous. He told me how he knew something had been going on at the location for months.

He said he noticed irregularities when he came to the store to pick up the scratch-off tickets the business didn't sell. Tickets were often returned not connected to their pack, and out of numbered order. He knew this was odd and it seemed to be happening every time he came to the store to pick up tickets. One time, he had even asked the clerk why the tickets weren't connected. She told him that the Asian customers who purchased the tickets were superstitious and wouldn't buy tickets containing certain numbers. He didn't think anything of it because he had previously worked in Asian communities in the Bay Area.

I asked the sales representative if he had ever told his supervisor about the irregularities. He admitted he hadn't said anything to anyone but had made a few notes in the lottery's computer system. I didn't press the issue. He and I both knew he should have said something. The sales representatives are underpaid for what they do to allow for bonuses to increase workflow. Those bonuses are based on their account sales. The bonuses were one of the only things keeping them afloat. His lack of action was part of a bigger problem that I had no control over.

The search warrant at the residence produced a ton of evidence. The team located additional pinned scratch-off tickets, and a secret ledger that contained the factual business record sales for the business's finances. We would later discover the owner was claiming a loss of over $40,000 every year on his taxes but was actually turning a profit.

It took about twenty hours over the weekend to process and secure all of the evidence obtained as part of the search warrant. In total, we recovered over three thousand pinned tickets, which were all assigned to the business. The evidence showed the family was taking the scratch-off tickets home when they received them. They would pin the tickets at their residence and bring them back to the business. The sister-in-law would then try to guess the VIRN on each ticket during her shifts. The lottery-funded the operation in the form of reimbursements they provided for winning tickets the business never paid out. The owner also received a commission on the sales.

The evidence made me think about something the sales representative had said to me about receiving tickets from the clerk that were out of sequence. Since almost every ticket we had recovered had been pinned, what if the lottery was giving the owner credit for losing tickets that were pinned? I began running billing and validation reports through the lottery's computer system. I compared the tickets the owner had received credit for to the validation reports for the packs the tickets were a part of. I discovered the lottery had consistently given the owner credit for pinned tickets, which led to him defrauding the lottery for over $10,000. This brought the lottery's total loss to over $90,000.

I contacted Ortiz and told him I had discovered another major flaw in the operation of the lottery. I explained how the lottery had given the owner credit for losing tickets that had been pinned. He repeatedly told me I was wrong because the system wouldn't allow credit for validated tickets. I asked Ortiz if he meant tickets that had been validated as losers or tickets that had been validated as winners. He told me the location couldn't receive credit for tickets that had been validated as losers. I sent him an email containing proof that the system was flawed and didn't recognize tickets that had been validated as losers. He took the information and forwarded it to lottery management. I was never contacted about this issue again, except to tell me they were "working" on it.

With this new evidence and the other evidence, I obtained of the wife claiming pinned tickets, I knew I had enough to not allow the owner to pin (pardon the pun) everything on his sister-in-law. My partners and I returned to Donut Queen. I arrested the owner and his wife. After we booked them into jail the same day, I felt I had righted a wrong. I knew that the system wasn't always fair, so it meant a lot to me any time I could balance it. Even just a little. (Galbreath, 14-986, 2014)

The investigation was a complete success. All three suspects pled guilty to multiple felonies and took plea bargains. The sister-in-law was the only one whose offenses were lowered to misdemeanors. The owner paid the lottery over $90,000 in restitution, which was one of the largest restitutions checks the lottery had received from a suspect.

The Ventura County District Attorney was proud of the case and issued a press release. The news media caught wind of it. For the first time in my career, one of my cases was the top news story in Los Angeles. LaBrie was upset when she got word of the press release. I was copied on an email thread that ordered me not to discuss the case with anyone from the media. LaBrie asked in the email who gave the District Attorney's office permission to issue a press release? This was the first time I realized our work in SLED was viewed as having a negative impact on the lottery by executives. They were angry and embarrassed. Brean and Tacchini wanted to honor me with a commendation at lottery headquarters. They were told "absolutely not," so I was quietly given a commendation at a range qualification. The picture of me holding my commendation was hidden on the shared drive. Only those who were present knew that management was happy with my work on the case.

(Wold, 2014).

CHAPTER 14

Craig Liquor

The lottery went on the defensive when it came to pinning after the Donut Queen case. A lottery employee began running reports to identify potential pinning, so the lottery could be proactive. The reports showed a large amount of potential pinning activity statewide, which meant investigators would need to address the problem immediately before the next large-scale loss occurred. Lottery management became concerned about potential interest from the news media. Lottery management began concealing information from the public, knowing that the lottery was subject to the Public Records Request Act. In all emails, we were told to use the term "altered products" instead of pinning. This was a result of the large amount of pinning cases being assigned statewide, which created concern for lottery management about the impact on their image. They believed that the emails would not have to be included in a request for information related to pinning because we were calling it "altered products." We would receive a stern reminder anytime we forgot to use the special code word in an email. This was usually through text or phone call. There was more concern about using the correct words than there was for actually addressing the crime.

The Donut Queen case sent a message to the lottery retailers in my region. Although the report showed multiple lottery retailers in the state were engaging in pinning activity, there were no cases assigned to Jeffra or me. The Santa Ana region had several retailers on the report and was dealing with a staff shortage, so I agreed to help out with the pinning cases in their region. It was quite stupid for me to offer to help because the drive to Santa Ana was almost three hours due to traffic. I believed the cases would be pretty easy to close because I had become somewhat of an expert on pinning. I was wrong.

I took on three pinning cases in Santa Ana. Two of them were just locations that were extremely busy because of gambling addicts constantly going in and out of the businesses with their scratch-off tickets. Conducting surveillance on these locations made me feel bad about my job for the first time. The locations were located in poorer communities in Orange County, which were predominately Hispanic. The people playing the scratch-off tickets looked more like addicts than people playing for fun. I watched countless people sitting outside of the stores vigorously scratching off the play areas of the tickets they had just bought. They threw the losing tickets on the ground. When they got a winner, they walked inside, purchased more tickets, and repeated the cycle. They left the area once they ran out of money. I saw no problem-gambling brochures when I went inside to do my undercover purchases. Despite obvious signs of addiction, the clerks weren't trying to stop the people from coming back into the store every few minutes to buy more tickets. I overserved the same cycle every time I visited the locations. It was heartbreaking.

The third location, Craig Liquor, wasn't as busy. I entered the store undercover and purchased a few scratch-off tickets. I brought my work computer with me because of the long drive. I ran the first ticket and discovered it wasn't pinned and hadn't been validated as a loser. The second ticket was a different story. It was validated as a loser several days before I purchased it. I inspected the ticket while sitting in my car. The lighting wasn't great, but I didn't see anything suspicious. The laminate scratch-off area looked intact. When I took a closer look at the bottom of the ticket, I discovered the ticket had, in fact, been pinned. The laminate on the ticket was a dark green. A crayon or something similar was used to fill in the scratch, making the alteration unnoticeable to the average customer.

The next day I began running reports on Craig Liquor at my office. I discovered someone at the location had been pinning scratch-off tickets for months. Scratch-off tickets were being pinned almost daily based on the reports. The VIRN on some of the tickets had been entered incorrectly over twenty times. It was far more apparent than my case at the Donut Queen, which had been almost six months ago. I knew the lottery clearly hadn't taken any action on my recommendation for a notification system when the VIRN was entered incorrectly multiple times. Had they done something to address the issue, I wouldn't be sitting in the parking lot looking at pinned tickets. At this moment, I knew I had caught a case that would piss off lottery management, but I had kind of accepted my role as a shit magnet by this point.

My partner went undercover into the location a few days later and purchased scratch-off tickets from a few of the games I had seen pinning activity on. She purchased several scratch-off tickets. All of them had already been identified as losing tickets prior to her purchase. She mailed me the tickets so I could log them as evidence. I received the tickets a few days later and inspected them closely. The scratch on each of the pinned tickets had also been concealed with a crayon or a pen. The suspect in this case was putting more effort into pinning the tickets than the suspects in the Donut Queen case.

I decided to do things differently on this case because the pinned scratch-off tickets had been purchased from two different clerks, neither of which appeared to be the owner. I wrote a search warrant for Craig Liquor, seeking scratch-off tickets, employment records, and the store's surveillance system. I was once again a tourist because I had never filed a case in Orange County. I entered the judge's chambers holding a box filled with reports and pinned tickets. The judge was a hard sell on issuing a search warrant because he knew absolutely nothing about the lottery. It took me three hours to explain the nature of the case and why I needed a search warrant. The judge finally agreed to give me one and happily signed the warrant.

Craig Liquor was a much smaller operation than the previous pinning case, so I put together a smaller search warrant team and invited the local police department. Lottery management gave us permission to temporarily suspend the location's contract and seize all lottery property. When we arrived at the business, it was only us because the local police department didn't bother showing up. After securing the scene and taking photographs, we began searching for evidence.

First, I searched the plastic dispenser on the counter and found multiple pinned tickets still attached to one another. We located several tickets worth a few thousand dollars set aside in a drawer. Ortiz assisted a lottery technician with securing the scratch-off ticket vending machine. Some customers felt more comfortable purchasing tickets from the vending machines because of the belief the machine is secured and maintained by the lottery, which it's not.

Ortiz called me over to the machine. He was shocked to find multiple pinned scratch-off tickets loaded into the vending machine. Neither of us had ever seen anything like this. The owner showed up while we were looking at the tickets. I asked him who loaded the tickets into the vending machine. He told me his son-in-law was the manager and would take care of stocking the machine. I asked him to call his son-in-law and have him come to the store. He called him, but he refused to come in, even though he was scheduled to work.

After serving the warrant I was contacted by an attorney who informed me he represented the family. He was a total and complete condescending tool who questioned my ability to serve a search warrant. I explained my peace officer powers and my level of training in identifying fraud and forgery. We discussed my authority to serve a search warrant and how solid the case was. He became a little friendlier and said he would be more than happy to speak with me should I need to ask the family any questions. I asked him if any member of the family had admitted to pinning scratch-off tickets. He told me they had not and "ordered" me to contact him before making any arrests. I told him to have a wonderful day and ended the call. I was once again dealing with a wealthy family who was protecting someone, but I wasn't sure who.

We recovered hundreds of pinned scratch-off tickets from Craig Liquor as a result of the search warrant. I started reviewing the surveillance footage from the system we had seized as evidence. I observed the son-in-law pinning tickets throughout his entire shift every day he worked. He would remove an entire pack of scratch-off tickets from the display and from the vending machine. He used a small object to remove the laminate covering the VIRN. He guessed the VIRN on each ticket, removing winning tickets once he correctly guessed the numbers.

The son-in-law used a crayon to fill in the scratch. He loaded the losing tickets he had pinned back into the plastic display case and the vending machine so they could be sold to unsuspecting customers. The suspect, the owner, and other employees all sold losing pinned tickets to unsuspecting customers. The surveillance system also caught my undercover partner purchasing tickets. The total loss to the lottery was just over $145,000. The suspect had been pinning tickets for almost two years, but obtaining reports for prior years was difficult because they were "archived" by the company that manages the lottery's computer gaming systems. The reports were inaccessible once they were archived.

I put together a solid case and made the drive back to Santa Ana to meet with another special prosecutor. I brought several boxes of evidence, including the footage of the son-in-law pinning tickets and using the crayon to cover his tracks. The special prosecutor was amazed to see something like this was occurring without the lottery discovering it sooner. The special prosecutor was an expert in white-collar crime and used a special enhancement for each of the incidents of fraud committed by the suspect. The suspect was charged with over ninety felonies. The special prosecutor told me the validation reports were a great piece of evidence because they showed the number of times the suspect entered the VIRN incorrectly. These reports demonstrated how committed the suspect was to defrauding customers and profiting from the fraud.

I took the case and the warrant to court to obtain a signature. Once again, a judge was shocked to find out the lottery had a police department, which was becoming a common theme for me. I explained the nature of the case. She was appalled that a clerk would defraud customers by selling them losing lottery tickets because she herself purchased tickets on a regular basis. She set his bail at $150,000, which was the highest bail I had received for a suspect.

One thing I did differently with this case was requesting a review of the source of any bail the suspect paid to be released. This type of request is usually granted when the lead investigator believes the suspect may use criminally obtained money to get out of jail. As a result, the suspect is required to provide the source of every dollar they use to post bail. This is done to ensure money is available should the court order the suspect to pay their victim restitution. The judge was happy to grant my request and attached it to the arrest warrant.

My partners and I drove to the suspect's residence the next day, which was the day before Thanksgiving. I knocked on the door and asked to speak with the suspect. His wife, who also owned a lottery retail location, said he wasn't home. She told me he had left town and wouldn't be back until after Thanksgiving. I told her I had a warrant for her husband's arrest and would come inside if I needed to, but I wanted to avoid doing so. She said he wasn't there, but she would call him and ask him to come home. I thanked her and went back to my car.

A few minutes later I got a call from a pissed-off attorney. He reminded me I was to contact him before making any arrests. I told him I forgot but really needed to arrest his client and wasn't going to leave until I did so. He told me he would call me back and hung up on me. A few minutes later, he called me back and told me his client would come outside and I wasn't to ask him any questions. I told him I had no questions and greatly appreciated his assistance. He once again hung up on me.

The front door to the residence opened. My suspect and another male came outside and walked over to my vehicle. The male told me the suspect had just gotten into town. I asked him if he teleported because I hadn't seen him arrive. He didn't think I was funny, but not everyone gets my sense of humor. We booked the suspect into the main jail in Santa Ana.

I finished writing my arrest report and began the long drive home. I received a call from a judge who wanted to know about the bail review request I had obtained. I provided him with the details during a lengthy conversation. The judge was completely satisfied with the justification and said he would probably get out of jail sometime next week because of the holiday.

The arrest made the local news and was covered by multiple stations. The suspect's booking photo was prominently displayed. I knew LaBrie would be pissed about the coverage. I was once again told not to discuss the case with the news media. I requested termination of the contract at Craig Liquor and his wife's location because of the potential threat the suspect posed to customers. Neither location was terminated.

The special prosecutor began contacting me because the suspect's attorney wanted to make a deal. Thinking on my feet because lottery management refused to do anything, I asked for a stipulation prohibiting him from working at any lottery retail location. The attorney allowed the stipulation. The suspect plead guilty to several felonies and was ordered to serve six months in jail, with another five years of probation. His lawyer gave me a restitution check for $146,000, which was made payable to the lottery. For this reason, I firmly believed the suspect had made much more from his crime than I was able to prove. (Dobruck, 2015)

After this case and the media attention, the lottery decided something had to be done to address pinning. Although implementing a notification system to notify SLED when a VIRN was repeatedly entered incorrectly made the most sense, other measures were approved. Lottery management decided the VIRN would be removed from all scratch-off tickets so they could be checked by simply scanning a barcode. I reminded Ortiz how valuable the VIRN was in the Craig Liquor case because of the evidence left behind. I suggested placing the VIRN in a different location on each scratch-off ticket. This method was used by other states and would preserve the evidence of fraud. I was one of several investigators who offered this suggestion. We were ignored.

Lottery management believed removing the VIRN would eliminate pinning. New scratch-off tickets were manufactured without a VIRN. The VIRN was replaced by a single barcode, which was located in the same location under the laminate play area. Lottery retailers only had to scan the barcode in order to validate a ticket and determine if it is a winner or a loser. This meant pinning cases would be difficult to prove because the lottery's computer system would only log one entry when the ticket was scanned. The digital fingerprint had been removed in favor of attempting to remove the temptation for fraud from lottery retailers and their employees.

A few months later I received a call from an LAPD detective. The new scratch-off tickets without the VIRN were being issued to lottery retail locations for several months by the time I received the call. The detective told me a business owner had one of his employees arrested for embezzling scratch-off tickets. The employee had been pinning tickets by exposing the barcode and scanning the tickets. The employee was able to embezzle a few thousand dollars' worth of tickets and had been selling losing tickets to unsuspecting customers.

I assisted the LAPD by running reports on the scratch-off tickets assigned to the business. The suspect had pinned some of the location's assigned tickets that still had a VIRN. I used this information to show the suspect was pinning tickets. The reports for the tickets he had pinned by exposing the barcode weren't so straightforward. The reports looked similar to others from a busy lottery retail location and would be shaky at best if they were introduced as evidence. The employee was only able to get representation from the public defender, so the validation activity for the tickets wasn't called into question. The suspect pled guilty and took a plea bargain.

I sent Ortiz an email containing pictures of the pinned scratch-off tickets and the validation report to demonstrate the new problem. I stressed the need to reinstate the VIRN because of the evidentiary value of the validation reports. He told me he would forward the information to lottery management. Nothing changed. The VIRN wasn't returned to the tickets. The lottery would eventually make it even more convenient for pinners because they added a "check a ticket" feature to the lottery smartphone app. This afforded lottery players the opportunity to check a ticket to see if it was a winner by scanning the code, which wasn't something the lottery is legally allowed to track. This change made pinning cases almost impossible to investigate. (Galbreath, 15-848, 2015)

CHAPTER 15

My 15 Minutes

March of 2015 was a difficult time for me. I was dealing with some personal issues and was still recovering from a bad car accident I had the previous year while on duty. One of my friends had been diagnosed with leukemia shortly after I came to work at the lottery. Aaron managed to beat leukemia but died from complications with chemo therapy that same month. I attended the funeral in Northern California. Jeffra had some evidence assigned to him that needed to be picked up from headquarters, so I decided to make a trip to Sacramento. It gave me an opportunity to pick up Jeffra's evidence and see my family.

I took the Friday off and worked a Retailer Compliance Program with Jeffra the Thursday before I left. I served as the undercover investigator and had a decoy ticket stolen from me at two different locations. The second location was a gas station in Palmdale. The manager took my $75,000 decoy scratch-off ticket and gave me $75, congratulating me on my big win. I took the money and left the store. I saved my video evidence and secured the $75 before heading home to switch cars. I drove to Sacramento later that night.

The next day, I arrived at headquarters. I saw old friends, hugged, and picked up Jeffra's evidence. One of the analysts approached me and told me she was on the phone with a store manager in Palmdale who thought they may have underpaid a customer. She said that the ticket may be a decoy scratch-off ticket based on the numbers she received from the caller. She asked me what I normally did in a situation like this. I told her to tell the caller we would send an investigator to the location to pick up the ticket sometime next week. I left headquarters and didn't think about the call again.

On Sunday, I attended Aaron's funeral. I really liked Aaron and was distraught about him losing his life at such a young age. He was only a few years older than me. The funeral reception was nice because I got to see some old friends. We shared stories some of us had forgotten about and had some laughs. I drove back to Los Angeles from the funeral reception. The store manager didn't call the lottery again, nor did the analyst send me an email providing me with the details from her call. With the funeral and everything else going on in my life, I didn't think about it again.

A few months later, I got a late-night call from Ortiz. He asked me if I had a decoy scratch-off ticket stolen from me in Palmdale. I told him I had, and he said, "Shit, I'm going to send you a link to a story." He told me to look at the link and see if I was the person in the photo. The link took me to a local news site. The person in the photograph was me wearing my brown polo shirt I found at a thrift store. The store manager grew concerned after the lottery never came to her store to pick up the ticket. She decided to go to the news media and release the surveillance footage in order to locate the winner.

I called Ortiz and told him I was, in fact, the person in the story. He told me he was going to call Brean and see if the lottery could get the story pulled before my picture was aired. Brean said there wasn't much we could do, so we would just wait until Monday. The story aired on the local news that night and started getting shared on social media. *Good Morning America* had aired the story and showed my picture that Sunday morning. The story went viral and was aired internationally on the BBC. The news media started contacting the lottery seeking comment.

The decision was made by Corporate Communications to identify me as an investigator so the country wasn't trying to locate a winner who didn't exist. I didn't agree with their decision because I realized it could impact my ability to do undercover operations in the future. Brean later told me that she and Tacchini fought to protect my identity but had no say in the final decision. Over time, I grew to appreciate the situation because I still got decoy tickets stolen from me. I even got to sign a few autographs. (Pamer, 2015)

CHAPTER 16

Powerball

In September of 2014, a Powerball ticket was sold at a lottery retail location in Rosemead, CA. The ticket matched five out of five numbers without matching the Powerball number, and it was worth over $1 million. The lottery released surveillance photographs of the individual they believed purchased the ticket in early 2015 because the prize remained unclaimed after almost six months. Unclaimed prizes are turned over to public education, but the lottery wanted to be fair and give the winner an opportunity to claim their prize.

Hung Nguyen was the man observed in the surveillance footage. He lived in Rosemead and worked in El Monte as an auto mechanic supporting a small family. Rosemead is a city located in Los Angeles County where, according to United States Census statistics, 14.5% of the residents live below the federal poverty level. Nguyen had been on vacation out of the country and had misplaced his ticket prior to leaving. He tried to find the winning ticket but was unsuccessful. He went to the lottery's Santa Fe Springs district office to try and claim his prize and told them he had lost the ticket.

Powerball rules were very specific and required the winner to be in possession of the actual winning ticket in order to claim the prize. California Lottery regulations permitted claiming a cash prize without the physical ticket, but this only applied to California-operated online games. In accordance with lottery regulations, a person claiming a prize without a ticket was, and still is, required to provide "substantial proof." Because Powerball was an interstate game with its own rules, the California Lottery denied Nguyen's claim.

At the time, Russ Lopez, the deputy director of Corporate Communications for the lottery, was interviewed by several different news stations reporting the story. In each story, he cited Powerball regulations and provided a silver lining, which was the prize money going to California's public schools. While it was disappointing, Nguyen couldn't claim a prize that would certainly change his life, but everyone could feel good about the schools getting additional funding. Despite his disappointment, he told everyone he would still buy lottery tickets. (Unknown, CBS Los Angeles, 2015)

On January 7, 2015, a Powerball ticket worth $1.9 million was sold in Century City. The winning ticket was a $20 wager which also matched five out of five numbers. There were several tickets sold within a few minutes of each other, but there was only one ticket that matched five out of five. Investigator Robert Forte was tasked with responding to the location and gathering information, which included attempting to retrieve surveillance footage of the winning ticket purchase. Forte discovered that the time on the surveillance system wasn't synchronized with the lottery and was about forty-seven minutes ahead. Forte took photographs of an individual who he believed may have been the winner but was unable to obtain any substantial evidence because of the inaccurate surveillance system.

The lottery had the photograph of a possible winner, which had been taken by Forte, but they didn't release it to the media the same way they had with Nguyen. Lopez had been quoted in the past saying that the lottery did not rely on surveillance footage alone to identify winners, but the lottery never released a photograph related to the purchase from Century City to the news media. (Various, 15-166, 2015)

On June 4 of 2015, Noam Kashanian walked into the lottery's Santa Fe Springs district office to claim the $1.9 million prize for the five-out-of-five Powerball ticket, which hadn't been claimed. Kashanian stated he was told by the Store Manager at the gas station in Century City that he was the winner because the lottery took his photograph. Ortiz and the office manager from Santa Fe Springs explained the regulations for Powerball to Kashanian and informed him he couldn't claim the prize because he didn't have the ticket.

Kashanian was in a much different situation than Nguyen. Kashanian lived in Beverly Hills. An Internet search using his name produces information about entries in poker tournaments and links to businesses, which list him as the owner. Kashanian hired an attorney, who contacted the lottery. I can't say I know what was discussed between Kashanian's attorney and the lottery, but I can state the facts regarding what occurred after the contact.

On June 25, 2015, at approximately 10:00 a.m., the Lottery Commission held a meeting. California Lottery employee Ed Fong appeared before the commission and presented a memorandum regarding amending Powerball regulations in California. This amendment included "updating" the existing claim procedures for individuals who didn't have the winning ticket in their possession. Fong said that Powerball sales had declined. He discussed the challenge of making the game more appealing to customers. After a back-and-forth with one of the commissioners, Fong got to the most crucial part of his presentation. In the transcript of the Lottery Commission meeting, Fong stated, " . . . with our other in-state games, if a player presents the lottery with substantial proof of a winning ticket, they can claim a prize without the actual game ticket. MUSL adopted this change, and California would like to adopt this change also here in California for Powerball."

As previously discussed, MUSL is run by state lotteries and is the driving force behind Powerball. MUSL was also the employer of Eddie Tipton, who was convicted of rigging several state lotteries.

The memo Fong provided to the commissioners about the Powerball regulation changes was from LaBrie. The section regarding claiming a prize without a ticket stated, "MUSL has also revised its rules to allow lotteries to permit ticketless prize claims if provided for by state law and regulations. The lottery currently has the discretion to allow ticketless claims for its in-state games if claimants can meet the lottery's rigorous standards of proof of ownership. If the proposed regulations are approved by the Commission, the lottery will also be able to offer this for Powerball claims as well."

If the regulation changes were approved, they would take effect immediately. Neither Fong, nor LaBrie made any mention of Kashanian or his attempt to claim a Powerball prize without a ticket. There was also no mention of backdating the approval to allow others, such as

Nguyen, the ability to claim a prize for a past game. The Lottery Commission unanimously approved the changes to the Powerball regulations. (LaBrie, 2015)

On June 25, 2015, at approximately 11:00 a.m., Kashanian returned to the Santa Fe Springs lottery office. Kashanian stated he was there to file a no-ticket claim declaration. Kashanian had been contacted by Corporate Communications employee Alex Traverso, who informed him that he could now claim the prize for the Powerball ticket he was previously told he couldn't claim. Traverso also informed Kashanian he would need to prove he was the rightful owner of the missing ticket. This was part of the "rigorous standards of proof" LaBrie had mentioned in her memo.

Field investigators didn't receive any formal training on a ticketless claim and what questions should be asked. As a result, the investigator did the best they could and forwarded their report to headquarters.

Brean reviewed any report involving a claim for a prize of $350,000 or more. She reviewed the claim and found multiple discrepancies, so she flew to Los Angeles and conducted a second interview with Kashanian. Brean gave Kashanian the opportunity to provide substantial proof he was in fact the rightful owner of the $1.9 million prize. Kashanian stated during the interview he had purchased a $6 ticket. The actual cost of the winning ticket was $20. Kashanian was unable to provide any substantial proof of being the actual winner.

Brean recommended denial of Kashanian's claim in the lottery's claim system. She also called Kashanian and explained why his claim was being denied. Glen Lewis, who was the lieutenant in charge of the unit that processes claims also recommended denial of Kashanian's claim. Brean and Lewis both stated Kashanian failed to provide substantial proof. They based their recommendation for denial on the Lottery Act and lottery regulations. (Various, 15-166, 2015)

California Lottery regulations can be accessed on their website in an effort to be "transparent." Here are three sections that are relevant to this claim:

Section 3.7.4 (a) of California Lottery Regulations states:

"Except as otherwise provided in these regulations, a valid, original Powerball ticket is the only proof of a player's selections and is the only valid instrument for Claiming a Prize or Promotional Award."

Section 5.3.4 (a) of California lottery regulations states:

"Pursuant to the Lottery Act, if a Claimant is unable to submit an original, winning ticket but does submit a timely Claim Form signed under penalty of perjury, the lottery may pay a Prize if the Claimant can establish by a showing of "substantial proof" that the ticket is a winning ticket and the Claimant is the Winner."

Section 5.3.4 (b) of California lottery regulations states:

"Pursuant to the Lottery Act, substantial proof means evidence that would permit the lottery to use established confidential validation and authentication procedures to validate a claim. Such evidence must be sufficient, relevant, and credible in light of all the circumstances. All prize payments based on substantial proof must be approved in advance by the Director." (Various, California Lottery , 2019)

The recommendation from Brean and Lewis to deny Kashanian's claim satisfied each of the sections I have previously mentioned. SLED has always been tasked with ensuring honesty, integrity, and fairness in the operation of the lottery. This claim was a perfect example of SLED personnel doing what they had been trained to do, and in Brean's case, had been doing for almost sixteen years. Although Kashanian wouldn't be receiving his $1.9 million prize, the money would end up going to the public school system, so once again, this was a win for education.

On August 11, 2015, LaBrie sent an email ordering Kashanian be paid based on "substantial proof," despite the investigation into his claim showing factual evidence that he hadn't provided substantial proof. (Various, Claims Comment, 2015)

The lottery didn't issue a press release about Kashanian's big payout. It was certainly a newsworthy story because he was the first California resident to receive a Powerball prize without having the actual ticket. The personnel at the Santa Fe Springs lottery office had taken a picture of Kashanian holding an oversized check with a big smile on his face, which was never released to the press.

Even if Kashanian had declined to speak with Corporate Communications, according to the lottery, his name, the prize, and the location where the ticket was purchased were still a matter of public record. In a *San Francisco Chronicle* interview in 2016, Traverso specifically indicated that the information on winners had to be made public so that people "know there are winners every day." The Kashanian claim is the only one I know of that didn't involve a press release for a big winner in my entire career with the lottery. (Gutierrez, 2016)

The decision to pay Kashanian didn't sit well with Brean, Tacchini, or Lewis. Brean filed an internal complaint against LaBrie for paying a claimant in violation of lottery regulations. Lewis filed an anonymous complaint with the California State auditor. Tacchini wrote a complaint to Kamala Harris, who was the California Attorney General, requesting an investigation into LaBrie's misconduct and the actions of lottery management. The California government code specifically required Tacchini to report any alleged violation of any law related to the operations of the California State Lottery to the attorney general and law enforcement. Tacchini followed the law as required and later submitted a written request for assistance.

In the request, Tacchini specifically outlined LaBrie's violation of the law and lottery regulations. Tacchini asked Harris, whose office had a law enforcement branch, to open an investigation of the lottery, lottery management, and LaBrie's actions. (Tacchini, 2016)

Shortly after LaBrie's directive to pay Kashanian, Brean was placed on Administrative Time Off (ATO). LaBrie requested an investigation into Brean by the California Department of Justice, which was overseen by Harris. Brean would ultimately be terminated for her complaint and attempt to do the right thing. I will share the fate of Tacchini shortly. (Helen Brean V. The California State Lottery, 2016)

LaBrie made changes to the way questionable claims investigations were handled. The lottery's legal division began reviewing every claim an investigator recommended for denial. It was made clear to SLED that the decision to pay or deny a claim would come from LaBrie and legal. Investigators were given no information about what was occurring, but SLED was starting to fall apart. Tacchini continued to try and support investigators and SLED as best he could, but we all knew something was wrong.

Ultimately, a man from Rosemead was denied a large prize under the same circumstances as a man from Beverly Hills. Nguyen's claim had far more substantial proof than Kashanian's, but the lottery didn't give him the same consideration. The rules weren't changed for Nguyen.

CHAPTER 17

My Most Important Case

In December of 2015, the accountant for a Valero gas station in Sherman Oaks discovered a serious discrepancy in the way the lottery was billing the location for scratch-off tickets. The scratch-off ticket bill had climbed almost 300%. The bill wasn't balancing out because the sales for the scratch-off tickets didn't match the bill. The bill showed the location was being billed by the lottery for entire packs of scratch-off tickets, but the location didn't appear to be receiving any money from customers.

The accountant and the owner resided in New York. The business was managed by the owner's niece, who hadn't noticed anything out of the ordinary because she believed the cost of the scratch-off ticket packs would balance out from the sales commission. The niece and the accountant began calling the lottery when the cost didn't balance out from commissions. There were several heated discussions between the business representatives and the lottery's revenue collections division. The niece accused the lottery of stealing from the business because the loss was now over $100,000. As usual, there was no regard or understanding for the amount of fraud occurring within the lottery. Revenue Collections told the niece that it appeared someone in the store was embezzling scratch-off tickets, not thinking for a moment that it could be the niece. The arguments continued for days before Revenue Collections finally asked SLED to get involved.

I was assigned the case in January of 2016. Almost two years after working my first embezzlement case. I started my investigation by running billing reports for the business. I compared the billing reports to the validation attempt reports for the scratch-off ticket packs. The packs contained suspicious validation activity which was identical to every embezzlement case I had worked. The major difference was the obvious change in the billing activity at the business. I was once again investigating a major loss, which could have been prevented, had the lottery implemented a notification system for scratch-off tickets.

The business had an average weekly bill for scratch-off tickets of 4–6 thousand dollars. The bill stayed the same for the one-year period I reviewed. In October of 2015, the bill started climbing significantly by several thousand dollars each week. I even found one week where the scratch-off ticket bill was just shy of $20,000. I checked the scratch-off tickets currently assigned to the business and the ones they had recently been billed for. The location was being billed for ticket packs that had only been active for a few days, which wasn't a normal occurrence.

It's important to know that lottery retail locations are billed based on individual lottery games, which are separated into different categories for scratch-off tickets and online games. This means factors such as a large jackpot for Powerball don't affect the bill for a retail location. Retail owners are billed differently for online games and scratch-off tickets. Any lottery employee looking at sales and billing should be able to notice a significant problem based on their training and experience.

Jeffra was heavily involved in my investigation and was helping me in any way he could. He was curious and asked me who the sales representative was for the location. I looked up the representative and saw it was the same one from Jeffra's case in 2013. I checked the comments section for the retail location and saw note after note from the representative talking about the amazing increase in sales at the location. The representative said he was going to congratulate the business owner. Once again, the sales representative didn't contact his supervisor, even though he noticed a significant increase in the business.

Tickets from Valero were being validated and paid out in large volumes at the same three locations in Reseda, which were several miles away from Sherman Oaks. The tickets were being validated as winners or losers on a self-check terminal prior to being cashed out at the same three locations. Tickets from Valero were being checked at the same locations starting in October of 2015. There was a clear pattern that was easy to document.

Jeffra and I met with the owner's niece. She told me she believed she knew who the employee was stealing tickets. She hired Assraf in October of 2015. He had worked at lottery retail locations for years and came highly recommended by a nearby lottery retail owner. She told me she believed Assraf was trustworthy, so he primarily worked the overnight shift by himself, where he had little to no supervision.

The owner's niece started reviewing the store's surveillance footage after she realized it was probably an employee that was stealing from the business. She gave me a thumb drive that had surveillance footage from the business during shifts where she saw Assraf stealing.

I watched the videos and saw the suspect place a yellow towel on the counter. He would remove several scratch-off tickets from the plastic display. He had expensive taste, so he would choose the higher-priced games. He placed the tickets on top of the yellow towel. He wore a gray hooded sweatshirt each time he stole from the business, which seemed to be his trademark. Assraf would "take the trash outside," sometimes waiving a black trash bag at the camera so the viewer knew he was taking out the trash. The camera outside of the business rotated. He would walk toward his car, timing his movements based on the camera rotation. You would never see him placing the yellow towel in his car.

I obtained Assraf's information from the owner's niece. He resided in Reseda, a few blocks away from the locations where the tickets were being checked and cashed out. My partners and I began going to each of the locations to review the surveillance footage. One of the owners told me he knew why we were there. Assraf would come to his store every few days with several tickets. He always had them in a stack and would cash in multiple winning tickets for several thousand dollars at a time. The owner would even make him coffee. Assraf told the owner he bought tickets all the time and made thousands, so he kept buying. The owner said he thought it was odd but didn't care because he was getting a commission for cashing out all of the winning tickets. This was a typical response from lottery retail owners when asked why they didn't report suspicious activity they thought may be criminal.

I watched the surveillance system for the store and positively identified Assraf. He had a stack of scratch-off tickets every time he walked into the store. He would separate the tickets into two stacks. He would hand one stack to the owner to cash out and would begin checking the other stack on the self-check terminal. On some days, when the owner was helping customers, he would let Assraf come behind the counter and check the tickets on the store's lottery computer. Assraf would check the tickets and set aside the claim receipts for the winners. Assraf would give the winning tickets to the owner once he was done helping customers and receive his cash.

I was able to obtain a large amount of video evidence, which made the case a slam dunk. I began adding up the loss to Valero and the lottery for the three and half months Assraf was stealing scratch-off tickets. The total loss to both was over $200,000. Assraf made over $90,000 from cash prizes alone. One of my partners, Robin Chan, even found two scratch-off tickets stolen from Valero worth over $2,000 Assraf had claimed with the lottery. We pulled the claim forms and saw Assraf had lied about being employed by a lottery retail location.

As previously discussed, the lottery doesn't require a background investigation on employees who work for lottery retail locations. Retail owners aren't required to give the lottery any information on the employees they hire or fire for misconduct either. The lottery could have flagged Assraf's claims for investigation a month and a half earlier had there been some sort of requirement for the information in place. It would also prevent an arrested employee from working at another lottery retail location after stealing tickets from their employer, or from a customer. There was even a case where the reporting party for scratch-off ticket embezzlement was a store manager who was a suspect at another lottery retail location for the same thing.

The case caused a lot of concerns for Jeffra and me because it was another preventable loss. Once again, I told Ortiz the lottery had to do something to address the scratch-off ticket issue. Jeffra also contacted headquarters and said the same thing, again. Jeffra was told that a consulting firm was being hired to help predict when a retail owner would go NSF. The "psychic" firm couldn't predict a loss at a retail location such as Valero because the owner had enough money through various business ventures to never go NSF. The only way to prevent large-scale loss such as this one would be to implement a notification or flagging system that would contact SLED when such an obvious increase in scratch-off ticket sales occurred.

Yet again, the problem wasn't going to be fixed, so I returned to the task at hand. I took my case to the district attorney, who filed several felony charges against Assraf. I obtained a warrant for Assraf's arrest and was able to get a bail review request granted. I asked Tacchini and Olsen for permission to arrest Assraf. Olsen was promoted to acting field chief because Brean was still off on paid leave pending investigation. Olsen had told me how much scrutiny SLED was under from the legal division, which was now being overseen by LaBrie. Governor Brown had appointed someone else, and LaBrie wasn't selected as the deputy director of the lottery. Olsen gave me the greenlight to arrest Assraf.

Jeffra, Chan, and I drove to the Valero Gas station where Assraf was scheduled to come in for work. We had already made arrangements with the owner's niece to have another employee ready to cover his shift.

The three of us entered the station's back office and took Assraf into custody. He was arrogant and pretended to not speak English. He had over $1000 in his possession, which he claimed was to pay his rent, even though it was the middle of the month. We transported Assraf to a local Sheriff's substation where I booked him for his warrant. Assraf remained in custody for a few months because of the bail review request.

Assraf eventually pled guilty and took a plea bargain. His attorney disputed the amount of restitution ordered by the court, so a restitution hearing was ordered. The owner's niece and I were the only two witnesses who had to testify. I was on the stand establishing the figure I came up with for over an hour. The defense attorney refused to acknowledge the large loss because of the belief the lottery should have known about the loss early on and had no way to prove the amount of loss I was alleging. I felt like a rock star because I was able to counter every allegation the defense attorney made.

The judge ordered Assraf to pay the entire amount and even added on a little extra. I got a high-five from the district attorney and handshakes from some other attorneys who were watching me on the stand. The district attorney, the owner's niece, and I left the courtroom. She thanked me for everything I did, even though we butted heads a few times on how to investigate the case. Then, she told me something that made me feel like my career was complete.

Assraf had been physically abusing his wife and children and had been for quite some time. His wife was terrified of Assraf and wouldn't leave him because she didn't think she could escape. While Assraf was in jail, he couldn't satisfy the bail review request because nobody was trying to bail him out. His wife packed up her family's belongings, took her children, and got away. Assraf was in no position to stop her, so she was no longer scared. My silly little lottery case actually made a difference in someone's life.

I thanked her for telling me and walked to my car. I sat in my car and couldn't stop myself from crying because I felt like I had done something truly important for the first time in my lottery career. I sent Tacchini and Olsen an email thanking them for letting me make the arrest and told them what had happened. Their responses are something I will always treasure and keep to myself. (Galbreath, 16-66, 2016)

CHAPTER 18

Tacchini

I took a trip to Sacramento in March of 2016. I stopped by headquarters to say hello to a few people who I hadn't seen in a while. I spoke with Olsen and Tacchini, who both looked worn down. Tacchini invited me into his office and closed the door. He told me that he was sorry that morale was suffering within the division. He said there were forces within the lottery that didn't appreciate the work of SLED and were doing things he didn't agree with. He told me to go back to Los Angeles and tell my partners they still had his support.

Hugo Lopez had been appointed as the deputy director of the lottery by Governor Jerry Brown. LaBrie was returned to the position of chief deputy director, which was the position she held when she was originally appointed by Governor Brown in 2012. LaBrie already had Brean investigated over her complaint about the payment made to Kashanian and wasn't a fan of SLED. LaBrie's position meant she would oversee the legal division, which had become heavily involved in scrutinizing SLED.

Tacchini tried multiple times to meet alone with Lopez to discuss his concerns about LaBrie and Legal. LaBrie would show up and sit in on every meeting he scheduled. The Kashanian case was one of the reasons Tacchini wanted to speak with Lopez alone. He firmly believed LaBrie and legal were violating lottery rules and regulations. Their actions were misappropriating public funds which should have gone to public education. This was done to simply avoid perceived liability and bad press.

Tacchini and other employees at headquarters created an Excel spreadsheet documenting each claim that had been referred to SLED for investigation. The spreadsheet included the reason for the investigation and the eventual decision made by legal to pay or deny the claim. Around the same time, lottery management seemed concerned with the potential discrepancy between recommendations made by investigators in the internal claims system and the decisions made by Legal and Lopez. I received an email from Ortiz indicating that we were no longer permitted to make a determination regarding a claimant appearing to be the rightful owner of a ticket and were prohibited from making a determination on a claimant being paid in our official reports. We were directed to simply document the investigation being completed and forward it to our supervisor for review. (Ortiz, 2016)

The comments made on a claim in the lottery's claim system, emails, investigator's reports, and the decision made by Lopez and legal, were all subject to the Public Records Request Act. It would raise questions if an investigator were to disclose something such as a retail owner admitting to discounting, and Lopez or legal making the decision to pay them anyway. It was obvious the concern of being audited was the driving force behind the directives we were receiving. This made me believe that lottery management knew what they were doing was wrong.

In May of 2016, Tacchini received a response from Kimberly McCrickard on behalf of Kamala Harris indicating the State Department of Justice wouldn't investigate his complaint. McCrickard stated that the California government code required the deputy director of SLED to notify the "appropriate law enforcement agency" and the state attorney general. McCrickard further suggested Tacchini contact Sacramento County authorities to investigate the potentially criminal acts of a California government official because the attorney general's office would only investigate if all other resources were exhausted. She also stated that Sacramento County was responsible for the investigation of crimes that occur within their county. None of this was accurate because the attorney general's office wasn't precluded from investigating a state agency for misconduct or potentially criminal actions. Local law enforcement rarely, if ever, investigated misconduct on the part of a state entity. (Harris, 2016)

Tacchini was relieved of duty by Jerry Brown around the time he received the response from Harris' office, even though his actions were protected by the California Whistleblower Protection Act. Tacchini had no recourse to pursue a wrongful termination case because he'd been appointed to his position by the governor. SLED found out Tacchini was no longer with the agency through an email from his assistant, which he had her send on his behalf. Tacchini wasn't able to send it himself because his computer access was taken away after he was told he was being terminated from his appointment.

CHAPTER 19

Rigging the Game

SLED Investigators used a variety of computer systems and files to do their jobs. This included a claim/ticket tracking system, a report writing system, and shared files. The interesting thing about the shared files was that anyone could access them unless a particular folder was limited to management-level access. If you stumbled upon one of those files you weren't permitted to access, the computer would display a pop-up window that said you didn't have access to the folder. One of my favorite files was the SLED shared file because it contained photos, past news articles, and other fascinating file folders which were fun to look through when there was some precious downtime.

I stumbled across one of these files around the time Tacchini was removed from his position. The title jumped out at me because it was called, "1LOTTERY CLAIM Master Legal Review Claims Log." I wasn't aware it was the Excel spreadsheet that SLED personnel working at headquarters had created to track claims being investigated by SLED and referred to legal. In retrospect, the title should have been a dead giveaway, but I had access to the folder and was curious what was on the list. In reviewing the list, I saw several of my own cases. Among other information, the list contained report numbers and the final determination regarding the payment of the claims.

One of the first claims that jumped out at me was a claim for a ticket worth $5,000. I located the associated report and read through it. The ticket in question was claimed by the daughter of a lottery retail owner. While being interviewed by an investigator, the daughter admitted she hadn't purchased the ticket she was claiming. The ticket had been "discounted," and as a result, the investigator recommended denial of her claim. The outcome of this claim was quite disturbing because Hugo Lopez ignored the recommendation of the investigator and paid the lottery retail owner's daughter anyway. (Various, 1LOTTERY CLAIM Master Legal Review Claims Log, Various)

As I continued to go down the list, I saw case after case of the legal division and/or Lopez ignoring the recommendation for denial from investigators. Lottery retail owners who admitted to purchasing tickets from customers were now receiving payments with no repercussions. It was now apparent to me what had been happened with Tacchini, Brean, and SLED. Not only was lottery management rigging the game to allow individuals who were not eligible to receive payments and get paid, but those who spoke up were being removed. For the first time, I began contemplating becoming a whistleblower.

The thought frightened me. Speaking up as a public employee, especially one in law enforcement, is frowned upon. You are taught in the academy to speak up. As a state employee, you agree to come forward if your employer is engaging in fraud, waste, or abuse on an annual basis. History has not been kind to whistleblowers. There are countless stories of individuals being fired, arrested, or fleeing the country after speaking up when they saw something they knew was wrong. I put my thoughts about whistle-blowing on the backburner and continued to move forward. There wasn't a doubt in my mind the day would come when I would need to make the decision to keep quiet or do something to make things right.

CHAPTER 20

AAA With a Badge

By now, you're probably aware that I don't have the best relationship with the CHP. While I respect the job of CHP officers and appreciate their efforts to keep roadways safe, I think they should stick to what they know best. One of the main issues with the CHP and the state of California is the fact that the state does not have an independent law enforcement agency. When the State Police and the CHP merged in 1995, the CHP assumed all of the responsibilities, which had previously been assigned to the state police. This included assisting state law enforcement agencies with command coverage when requested. It hasn't been uncommon since 1995 for CHP lieutenants and captains to assume the management of state agencies such as the Department of Motor Vehicles and the Department of Alcoholic Beverage Control. This normally happens after some sort of command staff shake-up within the organization, which was exactly what was happening with SLED. The deputy director of SLED had been removed, the assistant deputy director had resigned, and the field chief had been fired.

While I can't speak to the circumstances surrounding the departure of the assistant deputy director, I can say that both Tacchini and Brean were fired for speaking up about the lottery's pattern of misappropriating public funds and violating state law. It was apparent that lottery management wanted SLED to be seen and not heard. Lottery management was running the lottery like a private business with no oversight.

On May 26th, 2016, the Lottery Commission agreed to an interagency agreement with the CHP to fill leadership positions for two years with a price tag of $1,647,483.84. This amount was $706,985.30 more expensive than the salaries of the individuals who previously held the positions. I actually calculated the cost difference through a website that listed the salaries of all California public employees. I was able to come up with the figure by comparing the salaries/benefits of former SLED management to the salaries/benefits listed for the CHP personnel. The information was contained in a memo LaBrie provided to the Lottery Commission when requesting approval of the agreement. This was $706,985.30 being taken away from public education because of a "critical need" lottery management created by punishing whistleblowers. (Various, Transparent California)

James Libby, Aaron Goulding, and Kelly Dixon were selected to fill the vacancies within SLED. It was announced Libby, the new deputy director, would be traveling to each of the area offices in the coming weeks to introduce himself and meet the investigators. At this point, SLED investigators were receiving directives from lottery management, which were making the law enforcement aspect of our jobs impossible to complete. We received direction from lottery management to not transport individuals we arrested in our state vehicles, to keep our badges and firearms concealed when we were at the office, and to refer our criminal cases to local law enforcement.

There was no question that SLED was going in a different direction. It bothered me because I still believed in the oath I had taken when I was sworn in. The lottery was misappropriating public money and paying individuals who had committed fraud on a consistent basis. I felt completely helpless. The people who hired me were gone. Ortiz was useless because he was a yes-man, and lottery management had made what would happen to those who spoke up quite clear. I decided I would make one last effort to fix the problems internally when Libby came to my office. Libby was a peace officer. As a "cop," he would have to be reasonable when confronted with the violations of the law being committed by the lottery. He was also an employee of the CHP, the state police, so he would have no loyalty to the lottery. Rather than sit quietly and listen to his sales pitch, I was going to going to be brutally honest.

Libby informed us via email he would be meeting with Jeffra, Chan, Ortiz, and myself. It was a closed-door meeting in my office. After the introductions and a teleconference, I was told I had the floor. Jeffra and I took turns telling Libby that we had evidence the lottery was misappropriating public funds. We cited examples of claimants who were being paid despite lying on claim forms and admitting to discounting. We discussed the lack of a red flag notification system, which could prevent large-scale losses. We brought up legal interfering with investigators doing their jobs and the fact that the law enforcement aspect of our positions seemed to be getting phased out. Libby responded by telling us that we were wrong about legal because they were doing what was best for the lottery. Libby also said that we didn't need to arrest people. Libby then said something which would stick with me. He looked me in the eyes and said, "I will happily put it in writing so you can motherfuck me for the rest of your career."

Libby was arrogant and didn't impress me. After establishing his dominance, he made a statement that told me how he was going to lead SLED. Libby told us that we needed to look at ourselves as "corporate loss prevention." Libby said we had what Xerox loss prevention wished they had because we were peace officers. Libby closed with a statement I will never forget: "The lottery is more like a corporation, and all corporations have shrinkage." Public money, especially money that would otherwise go to schools, was not something I could view as shrinkage. I now knew what I had to do and that I would have to face my fears. It was time to become a whistleblower. (James Thomas Jeffra V. California State Lottery, 2019)

CHAPTER 21

Another Big "Winner"

On June 27, 2016, Rodolfo Valderrama came to the San Francisco lottery office to file a claim for a $750,000 winning scratch-off ticket. Valderrama told Corporate Communications he had gone into a convenience store with two of his workers. He purchased a scratch-off ticket, which he scratched off. He checked the ticket at another location and realized that he had won $750,000. He was asked by the Corporate Communications representative if he was going to share his winnings with his employees since they had all gone into the store together. Valderrama said he wasn't going to share because he usually gives his guys bonuses.

When Valderrama met with Lottery Investigator Todd Kyle, his story was different. Valderrama admitted that he wasn't present when the ticket was purchased, nor did he scratch off the ticket. He said the ticket had actually been purchased by one of his employees, who had also checked the ticket on his own to see if it was a winner. Valderrama said he wasn't present when the ticket was checked. Valderrama claimed to have paid for the ticket his employee purchased but wasn't present when the ticket was purchased or scratched off.

Lottery regulations define a "winner" as a player, who is not a disqualified person, who legally acquires a winning ticket and owns it at the time it is determined to be a winning ticket either by a draw or by scratching the play area. Lottery regulations also state that a winner need not have purchased the ticket, but the winner has to claim the prize. This means when you have possession of the ticket, even if you didn't buy it, and you discover you are a winner by scratching off the play area, you are the winner. It's very black and white. Nothing in the regulation is really left open for interpretation. In this case, Valderrama had no legal claim to the $750,000 he was attempting to collect.

Kyle spoke with Valderrama's employee, Juan Mendez, a short time later. Mendez said he and his co-worker had been dropped off at a convenience store by Valderrama, who had given him some money to purchase a scratch-off ticket and some food. Mendez purchased the ticket, scratched off the play area, and realized he was a big winner. Mendez said he checked the ticket at two separate locations to confirm it was a winner. He called Valderrama and told him about the winning ticket, and would eventually meet up with him to hand over the ticket.

Kyle met with Mendez on two occasions. During the second meeting, Kyle explained the definition of a winner per lottery regulations to Mendez. Kyle told Mendez he was the lawful owner of the ticket, not Valderrama, so he would need to claim it. Mendez told Kyle he didn't have a social security number and wasn't a United States citizen. Because of this, he did not want to file a claim and insisted that the ticket belonged to Valderrama.

I read the report prepared by Kyle when I saw this claim listed as paid despite a recommendation from Kyle that it be denied. Kyle pulled no punches in his report, documenting the untruthful statements made by Valderrama and the fact that all of the evidence showed that Mendez was the actual winner. It also cited the specific lottery regulations and government codes that required the denial of Valderrama's claim.

Attached to Kyle's report was a supplemental report from Dixon, which stated he had discussed the denial of the claim with the lottery's legal division. Dixon stated he was recommending that Valderrama's claim be paid. Dixon provided no explanation for his decision to ignore regulations and laws.

The lottery paid Valderrama $750,000. The payment was made despite knowing Valderrama's entire statement to the lottery was a lie. Corporate Communications issued a press release with Valderrama's picture and his fictitious account of what had occurred. Had Valderrama's claim been denied and Mendez didn't file a claim, the $750,000 would have gone to the unclaimed prize pool. The prize would have been dispersed to California's public schools.

You may be asking yourself why I care so much about this particular claim? I care because the State of California champions itself as being a sanctuary state. I personally don't care about someone's citizenship status and never have. I grew up in areas where my neighbors were undocumented, and I have been lucky enough to call some of them family. Because of my personal experience, I also understand the reluctance to trust the system. At the same time, I'm not a fan of trusting someone's boss with making sure that the person who was the actual winner of a large prize gets their share, especially when the rightful owner of the ticket has no recourse to collect anything he may be owed.

The worst part about all of it was knowing how much that money would have changed Mendez's life. Once again, the lottery failed to protect one of its most venerable customer bases. They not only paid someone who wasn't the rightful owner of a ticket, but they paid someone who had control over the person who was. (Kyle, 2016)

CHAPTER 22

Blowing the Whistle

I knew Libby and Dixon had no interest in addressing the issues brought to their attention after a few weeks of working for them. I didn't know much about Goulding because he didn't seem to be to have an interest in being involved in any of the decision-making. It was clear to me the marching orders the CHP personnel had received was to do what they were told based on Dixon's actions throughout the Valderrama case and the statements made by Libby.

In August of 2016, I received a call from Ortiz regarding the report I had written on the owner of the donut shop in Panorama City. Ortiz told me Dixon had reviewed the case and wanted me to change my recommendation on the filing of criminal charges. Ortiz said Dixon wanted me to change my recommendation on the case to a denial of the claim and probation for the retail owner. I told Ortiz I was surprised about this case now being a concern considering it had been waiting on his approval for almost eight months. I told Ortiz I wasn't comfortable changing my recommendation because I was concerned about the retail owner continuing to target vulnerable individuals. I believed he should be arrested. Being the reasonable person I was, I told Ortiz that I would change my recommendation provided Dixon sent me an email ordering me to do so because I wouldn't be insubordinate. Dixon either lacked the courage to put his request in writing or he didn't want a paper trail. I'll never know which one.

The next day I received a call from Ortiz. He said he discussed my concerns with Dixon and they had come up with a solution. I would separate the claims case from the criminal actions of the owner and close it out as being referred to my supervisor. Dixon said that I could open a new criminal case on the owner, but I would need to wait until Dixon returned from his vacation. I knew at that moment that a new criminal case would not be opened and the owner would get paid for the ticket he was claiming. Ortiz spent the next hour on the phone with me telling me how to rewrite my report. He went through the report line by line. He had me remove sections that referenced the owner's criminal actions and replace them with more ambiguous sentences. By the end of our phone call, my twelve-page criminal report had become a one-page claims investigation report which was mostly inconclusive. By writing my report in an ambiguous way, and excluding the incriminating statements made by the suspect, lottery management could pay him even though the ticket wasn't his.

After hanging up with Ortiz, I felt as if my chest was tightening and realized that I was extremely stressed out. It was the first time I felt like I was having a panic attack. I closed my office door, turned off the lights, and lay on the ground in the darkness. I began reflecting on my law enforcement career up until this point. I had survived fights with countless people who were bigger than me. I had survived a near shooting. I had responded to countless stressful situations. Here I was, having a panic attack over my spineless Lieutenant rewriting my report. At first, I felt ashamed of myself for letting it happen, but my shame quickly turned into anger because I had become a part of the behavior my employer had been engaging in. This disgusted me. I got up and went to the break room to grab a glass of water.

As I stood in the kitchen, I was drawn to the poster from the state auditor that proclaimed in large words "whistleblowers are protected." I took a closer look at the poster, which was an enlarged version of the brochure we received every year from Human Resources. One of the sentences said, "It is your responsibility as a government employee to report any type of fraud, waste, or abuse." I stood there for a moment reading the rest of the poster, especially the part about me being free from retaliation for whistleblower activities. There was ample evidence proving lottery management and now CHP personnel had been engaging in fraud, waste, and abuse. I copied the number and walked outside to the parking lot.

My heart was racing as I called the number provided for the state auditor. A voice on the other end answered. I identified myself as a lottery investigator and told the person on the other end that my employer had been misappropriating public funds. It appeared they were doing it for no reason other than potential bad press. I shared the story of Kashanian and the repercussions faced by SLED management who voiced their opposition. I told them I could provide reports that would substantiate my claims.

The person on the other end was very cold and didn't seem to care about any of my concerns. She asked me why I wasn't taking my complaints to a law enforcement agency to investigate the potentially criminal actions on the part of my agency management. I told her I was calling the state auditor because, based on their poster, and my annual notification email, it was my responsibility as a government employee. I asked if she could suggest a law enforcement agency to report the allegations to because the attorney general refused to investigate. She said she understood my concerns and would refer my complaint to an investigator who would possibly contact me. I ended the call and went back to feeling helpless. The agency responsible for taking complaints from state workers didn't seem interested in doing their job.

The next day, I had breakfast with Jeffra. I told him I had contacted the state auditor and reported lottery management for misappropriating public funds. Jeffra laughed and told me he had contacted them last month to report the lack of a red flag system and fiduciary negligence. I told him I liked the big words he used and was happy that I wasn't alone. I also said I felt we should do more but protect ourselves in the process. He asked me what I had in mind, and I told him we should write a formal complaint and tell them we're willing to testify. Whistleblowers were protected, and at this point, I was concerned about remaining anonymous because I didn't believe it would change anything. Jeffra said he agreed, and felt that I should write the complaint, which I should have seen coming. As we have established, Jeffra wasn't a big fan of writing reports, so I agreed. This would require gathering reports proving our allegations and putting pen to paper on the things we had witnessed. We were officially investigating our employer.

I pulled every applicable lottery regulation and state statute that was applicable to our complaint before I started writing. After naming all involved parties and witnesses, I dove into all applicable sections, which I defined in detail. I included the section and definition, ensuring each applicable one would be cited when naming the individual who violated it. I included every case I could think of which applied to Jeffra's complaint about the red flag system. I did the same with my complaints regarding the misappropriation of public funds—and illegal payments made to individuals who had committed fraud. I included our efforts to address multiple issues internally on several occasions and the lack of response. The complaint ended up being over twenty pages by the time I was finished. After receiving Jeffra's seal of approval, we began printing out the reports we had previously written and others that were relevant to our allegations. Because we had written the majority of the reports based upon our investigations and due to the fact that there were no restrictions on printing out your own reports, no red flags were raised. I used the term "reference" for each report I printed because I was using it as "reference" for a complaint to the state auditor.

The process of redacting the reports so no personal identifying information was released to another state agency was very time-consuming. I wanted to make sure we were bulletproof, so I took the extra precaution of redacting. The state auditor was legally allowed to receive confidential documents as part of a complaint, and their website says that it is very helpful to have copies of any documents that support what you are saying. In this case, we didn't think any document could prove our allegations any better than the actual reports we had completed following our investigations.

Jeffra and I put everything together into a packet and each signed the complaint. We discussed our game plan on mailing the complaint to the state auditor's office. It dawned on me that Brean had also gone to the state auditor and ended up getting fired anyway. I decided to float the idea of sending a copy of the complaint to someone else in state government. Jeffra and I thought about it and decided to involve our union since they would ultimately end up being involved if we were retaliated against. This seemed like a good idea since we were paying them monthly to watch out for our best interests.

To be clear, I never thought I would be in a situation where I needed to involve my union. As an investigator, I was a top performer who had the highest prosecution rate. I was considered an industry expert and had received several letters of commendation for my work. I honestly wasn't a fan of our union, or most police unions, because they seemed to only get involved in situations once someone was being fired. They would often brag in press releases that they had gotten personnel their jobs back. In my opinion, some of the reinstated personnel shouldn't be working in law enforcement based on their conduct, but it ultimately wasn't up to me.

I contacted the chief counsel for my union and voiced my concerns about everything that had happened, and was still happening. He told me there had been calls from other lottery investigators who had some similar concerns. I told him I really wanted to try to make things better but was concerned about a lack of action on the part of the state auditor. I asked him if he could recommend a particular state office, politician, or committee that could also assist in making changes to hold the lottery accountable by receiving our complaint. He said he could not recommend anyone and recommended I keep my concerns to myself. He brought up the potential for me to lose my job and my retirement. He suggested I go work for another state agency and forget about my complaint. Jeffra and I were on our own.

Our written complaint didn't only include the allegations of misconduct and misappropriation of public funds; it also included recommendations on how to fix the issues. We took special care to ensure we weren't simply bringing up issues without offering solutions. We recommended having SLED report to the Lottery Commission or the attorney general's office. We made the case that SLED should serve as independent auditors who safeguarded the integrity of the lottery. Our intention was to help make our agency better. We felt good about our complaint and the contents. (Jeffra G. R., 2016)

CHAPTER 23

Investigative Reporting

Jeffra and I knew we needed to take additional steps to protect ourselves after my conversation with the union. There was a chance nothing would really be addressed if we just filed our complaint with the state auditor. We knew Kamala Harris' office was useless, and the union offered no additional avenues. I suggested we take our story to the media but do it in a way that wouldn't involve us releasing any confidential information. A news reporter could get a leg up if they knew where to look, who they could talk to, and what to ask for.

The Los Angeles Times was my first call. I had read several articles written by one of their editors on misappropriation of public funds. I didn't tell him who I was but gave him the general story, which piqued his interest. He told me to call back in a few months because he was working on several stories. This wasn't really an option because Jeffra and I were both stressed. We wanted to file our complaint. It's hard to truly express the stress involved to be in possession of information that could potentially expose a multibillion-dollar entity that is engaged in gross misconduct. Especially when you have everything ready to send but haven't yet mailed it to anyone. Your mind wanders to dark places despite preparing yourself for the possible repercussions. There are plenty of stories of whistleblowers committing suicide. It's possible the individuals were stressed, and it's also possible they were a problem that needed to be dealt with. Every phone call or discussion, outside of those you trust the most, is a chance for you or your efforts to get derailed before any real action is taken

One of my favorite reporters was David Goldstein. He was an investigative reporter who loved exposing government corruption and confronting those involved head-on. When watching him, you thought he may get punched in the face by the individuals he was confronting, but he was also quite tall and looked like he could hold his own. One of my favorite stories involved him recording several Cal Trans employees who drove their state vehicles to a restaurant and spent hours drinking alcohol. Considering the amount of road construction in LA that was never completed, the story was infuriating. He confronted the employees as they were returning to their cars. He shoved a microphone in their faces after telling them what he had observed and asked for an explanation. They of course did not have one and scrambled to get away. His investigations were thorough, and he wasn't afraid to confront anyone, including Jerry Brown.

As previously mentioned, Goldstein had done an investigation into the lottery a year earlier, which involved questioning the number of claims submitted by retailers, which was a high number. The segment involved him going to several locations where the retail owners were claiming the majority of the large prizes at their stores. The piece ruffled a lot of feathers in the lottery community because he specifically went after some of the top sellers in California. I personally enjoyed the piece because I had had far too many encounters with lottery retail owners who were discounting, which was specifically discussed during the segment. One of the owners he confronted owned another shop I had raided with LAPD for illegal gambling. His shop had video slot machines and cash poker games in addition to lottery products. This was another retailer who was placed on retailer probation rather than losing their contract.

I called Goldstein and left him a message detailing my story and my desire to share it with him. Leaving my phone number was risky, but I trusted him based on his previous stories. He called me back a short time later, and we set up a meeting at the coffee shop up the street from my office. Jeffra and I met with Goldstein and shared our concerns. We told him we were taking our complaint to the state auditor but wanted to make sure that there was some sort of public knowledge about what was occurring. Our hope was to create an added layer of protection. We also wanted to generate enough public and political interest to ensure our complaint wasn't ignored the same way previous ones had been. Goldstein was extremely interested in telling our story and wanted to move forward. I explained that Jeffra and I wouldn't be able to do an on-camera interview because we were still employed by the lottery but mentioned Brean and Tacchini. Both were more than happy to go on camera.

Goldstein ended our meeting by saying I needed to be on camera to tell my story because it was compelling. He wanted Jeffra and me to be a part of the piece and offered to do our interviews in a dark room to conceal our identities. He would also disguise our voices. The idea appealed to the entertainer in me because I had watched a ton of those interviews and parodies of them. We told him we would think about it and get back to him.

The next day, Jeffra and I mailed our complaint to the state auditor. While it was a huge load off of our shoulders, there were other weights to replace it. We had individually reached out to several politicians who we thought would be interested in the complaints. This included senators and popular political figures. Members of public education funding committees, Republicans and Democrats who called for additional government oversight. Anyone with more political power than the two of us.

I went through the trouble of setting up a fake email account and used my personal cell phone number in the emails, which created stress, but the complaint was already on its way to Sacramento. I even used one of my resources who worked in the office of a Senator who was on a committee for public education, which included funding. I thought for sure having a friend who was a staff member in the office to share my knowledge of the misappropriation of educational funds would spark some interest. I was wrong. Nobody in office or any of the other politicians we contacted, seemed interested in discussing the matter. I was starting to think that the state was complicit, and both major political parties were just flexing as part of a dog and pony show. I would later realize this was the case.

Jeffra and I spent several days discussing appearing on Goldstein's segment. After multiple conversations and continued frustration with lottery management, we decided to participate in the story. Natalie drove us to the CBS studios on a Saturday morning in September. We went through the backlot and eventually arrived at the CBS 2 news studio. Goldstein gave us a tour and led us downstairs to a dark room. We both wore hats in an effort to disguise our bald heads. Jeffra wore his signature Native American ballcap. I wore a newly purchased fedora as a nod to my Uncle Tony and my grandfather, who had both passed away. They were an important part of my life and would smile knowing I did it to honor them. Going with the theme, I also thought it was very old-school detective to wear a fedora while spilling the beans.

Goldstein covered a range of topics during our interviews. Jeffra and I were very calculated and vague in our responses. While we wanted to add to the story, we didn't want to give our identities away by being too specific, nor did we want to say anything that could get us fired. Goldstein asked me if people were getting paid for prizes they shouldn't be. I said, "absolutely, and that has been occurring on a frequent enough basis that it is very alarming." I didn't mention the legal claim referral list or the retailers who were getting paid despite admitting to discounting during my interview. While I did mention illegal payments to Goldstein, it wasn't a part of the final piece, which was unfortunate because it could have shown the public a pattern of behavior from lottery management.

We spoke with Goldstein after the interviews in the studio lobby. He told us the piece was coming together. He had submitted public records requests to the lottery for information related to the Kashanian claim, which was going to create heartburn for lottery management. He also spoke to Brean and Tacchini, who agreed to sit down for on-camera interviews. While I was excited that the story was coming together, it made my anxiety worse because I knew lottery management would question why a reporter was looking into their skeletons. There was no turning back now. (Goldstein, CBS Los Angeles, 2016)

CHAPTER 24

One Last Trip

October of 2016 was one of the most stressful months of my life. Jeffra and I had submitted our complaint to the state auditor, Goldstein's report was in its editing stage, and the CHP management ordered a mandatory training meeting at lottery headquarters. Jeffra and I were scheduled for different sessions during different weeks to ensure coverage in Van Nuys. Chan was no longer with the lottery, and there was no indication a third investigator would be hired. This was a problem because I had a feeling there would be a lack of coverage in the next few weeks.

I choose to drive to Sacramento because it was my hometown and I would have an opportunity to see family during my visit. The drive also gave me the opportunity to do a lot of thinking about what may happen while I was in town, which wasn't a good thing in retrospect. I made the decision to not leave the first floor of the building, which was where the training was being held. This would prevent me from being cornered by someone in lottery management. Over the past several weeks I had become convinced that the lottery knew what I was doing.

This was probably a combination of stress, lack of sleep, and slight paranoia. I was also becoming defiant for the first time because Jeffra and I had established ourselves as whistleblowers with the state. I thought we were protected but still wanted to avoid any unnecessary drama until it was absolutely necessary.

The drive also gave me an opportunity to reach out to Brean. I told her I would be in town for the training session and asked if she would like to meet up for lunch. She loved the idea of meeting up for lunch, and offered to pick me up at headquarters as her own personal hello to lottery management. I also loved the idea and agreed.

The training sessions consisted of CHP/SLED management telling us how things would be done going forward. We were also treated to a feel-good portion on SLED's great relationship with legal. There was some noticeable tension between Lewis and the CHP personnel. At one point during a presentation, Dixon and Lewis got into a heated discussion. Lewis walked out of the training and didn't come back. I didn't get a chance to discuss the politics in headquarters with Lewis and wasn't going to go to the second floor to talk to him either. Dixon had an ego, and Lewis wasn't afraid to push back.

Later that day, Brean picked me up in front of headquarters. She pulled up in a bright red convertible and got out of the car to give me a big hug. Even though we were both involved in efforts to disclose lottery corruption to the public, it was the first time we had seen each other in over a year. She had never gotten an opportunity to say bye to everyone, and her departure was never formally announced to SLED.

During lunch, Brean told me about the details surrounding her termination. She was escorted out of the building by agents from

Kamala Harris' attorney general's office—the same agency Tacchini had asked to investigate lottery management. Brean was informed she was suspended with pay and was under investigation. She was ordered to stay at home during business hours, with the exception of her one-hour lunch break. While at home, she would see agents parked outside of her house conducting surveillance to see if she was complying with the orders. She was even followed at times. She would be accused of lying, conduct unbecoming of a peace officer, and other bogus accusations which arose from her recommendation for the denial of Kashanian's claim.

Lottery management asked the attorney general's office to conduct Brean's investigation despite SLED having internal investigators, who had previously investigated any internal issues. Having an outside entity investigate a member of SLED was unorthodox considering I myself had been a witness to a previous internal investigation, which was conducted by SLED investigators. I also found it odd that Kamala Harris denied a request to investigate lottery management, which included individuals appointed by the governor, but authorized an investigation by her agency into a mid-level manager for misconduct. Something didn't add up. At the conclusion of the investigation, Brean was terminated. The lottery moved forward with the termination despite the fact Brean had identified herself as a whistleblower. She went on the sue the lottery for wrongful termination and was ready for her day in court with a long list of witnesses. The lottery chose to settle her case, and the official record would reflect her retirement.

Brean's settlement didn't include the lottery removing any record of the investigation into her "misconduct" or the allegations they made to smear her reputation. The lottery also hadn't signed a non-disclosure agreement to bar them from making disparaging remarks or sharing information that should have been sealed following the settlement. As a result, Brean would find herself being denied law enforcement jobs she applied for, despite having the required qualifications. She had been labeled a whistleblower, so she was damaged goods. Because of the lottery's continued efforts to smear her name, she changed careers in retirement and found new success in another industry. I will always be thankful for the opportunity she gave me and would stand beside her before standing beside any of the individuals who replaced her.

As much as I enjoyed my conversation with Brean, hearing her share her story convinced me Jeffra and I would suffer the same fate. I didn't regret our decision because I knew we were doing the right thing, but I also knew that the stress was going to get worse. Brean dropped me off in front of headquarters and gave me a final big hug. She wished me luck. I went back inside and was greeted with a few dirty looks, which made me happy.

The next day of training involved more nonsense I knew was being presented in an effort to justify wrongdoing. Ortiz and one of the lieutenants from the Southern region were in my training group. Pete Araujo oversaw the Riverside and San Bernardino offices. He was a typical frat boy type who became a cop. I had no respect for him because I had heard of past homophobic jokes Jeffra had heard him make about Gutierrez, who had previously supervised me. I considered Gutierrez a friend and a great human being. I even went to his mother's funeral. Gutierrez never spoke badly about anyone, and he always did his job. While I had never seen or heard this type of behavior from Araujo myself, he often acted immature during group training sessions, so it wasn't something I would put past him. Araujo was a yes-man who did as he was told by lottery management, and was well-positioned politically. Having been a drama geek in high school, and knowing some amazing human beings who also happened to be gay, this type of behavior never sat well with me. Unfortunately, homosexuality is a common thing joked about and used as hazing in law enforcement. It's a combination of fear and ignorance, which could be a standalone book.

During a break, Araujo started walking around the room wearing a sweater that was several sizes too small. He stuck his chest out, bent his wrists, and began asking if we liked his sweater. Araujo asked this question while speaking with a lisp in a manner that was clearly playing up a homosexual stereotype. He told the room he had gotten the sweater from Gutierrez's office. The training was started back up before I could call Araujo out for being a piece of shit. I spent the rest of the day angry and wanting to tell him off, but all things considered, I decided causing a scene wasn't in my best interest at the moment. Araujo, like the rest of us, didn't know if Gutierrez was gay, but he clearly assumed he was. Seeing a "lieutenant" openly mocking and making insinuations about a peer was a level of immaturity and ignorance I had never witnessed firsthand before this training. I decided to write a formal complaint regarding his conduct once I left Headquarters.

On a more positive note, while in Sacramento, I got to spend time with several people I care about. I shared what was going on and what I suspected was going to happen in the coming weeks. I was completely overwhelmed by the support I had and left feeling I was even more ready to tackle what was ahead of me.

After returning to Los Angeles, I spoke to Ortiz about Araujo's misconduct during the training. I told him I wanted to make a formal complaint regarding the inappropriate and discriminatory behavior by a lieutenant. I described Araujo's behavior in detail to Ortiz and told him I expected an internal investigation. Ortiz met with me in person a few days later. He told me that he had forwarded my complaint to Dixon, who said he would "address" it with Araujo. Dixon later told Ortiz he had spoken to Araujo and told him not to behave that way in the future. I asked Ortiz if there would be an investigation into Araujo's behavior considering he was a lieutenant and acted in a discriminatory manner in front of his subordinates. Ortiz said what he told me was what he was told to say by Dixon, but I could push it over his head if I wanted to. Ortiz had no courage and was dismissive in a way that caught me off guard, even though it shouldn't have. I wasn't completely surprised because people who are well-liked tend to get away with being "spoken to" until their behavior escalates to someone getting hurt. Especially in law enforcement. I sent an email about the situation to my department union rep but didn't get any traction. With everything that was going on, I choose to let it go, but it still doesn't sit well with me. I should have done more and regret not pushing the issue. Ray, I'm sorry and will always remember the kind human being you are. Thank you for everything. (Galbreath, Formal Complaint-Email, 2016)

CHAPTER 25

The Big Reveal

Las Vegas was my home away from home. I love the city, the culture, and the sights. Halloween was my favorite time to visit Las Vegas, which is where I was in 2016. Goldstein sent me a text that I received while eating at a buffet. He informed me the first part of the story was going to air that night. Natalie and I spent the next several hours walking around the strip. We were in the Flamingo when the broadcast started. We sat down in a stairwell and streamed it on my phone.

The first story was about the Powerball claim that got Tacchini and Brean fired. He covered the difference in the time on the surveillance footage, the lottery regulations being changed, and the terminations of SLED management. He also covered LaBrie ordering payment based on substantial proof that didn't exist. What he didn't cover was the lack of the same response from the lottery for Nguyen, which was an important element to the story. There was no mention of the lottery calling Kashanian and telling him to come in and file a claim after they were contacted by a lawyer. The most powerful part of his segment was the statement provided by the lottery where they said they based their decision on the surveillance photo and were "confident it awarded the prize to the right person."

The lottery had officially contradicted itself by making that statement. Never mind the fact that when asked about surveillance footage by a reporter in January 2016, Lopez stated:

"It's supplemental, we've seen photos that have been wrong in the past . . . we don't want to make that mistake again." (Tadayon, 2016)

The lottery was now saying the surveillance footage proved the correct person was paid. The statement from Lopez was something I was going to point out when I was contacted by the state auditor as additional evidence of what we had reported. (Goldstein, CBS Los Angeles, 2016)

That evening Natalie and I used fake *Facebook* profiles to share the story on the *Facebook* pages of MULA and the World Lottery Association, which LaBrie constantly bragged about having level-four certification with. As an additional touch, I posted a link to the story in the comment section of several of the lottery's posts. It was petty, but by now I was fairly fed up with the nonsense.

The second part of the story aired the next night. The segment included the interviews he did with Jeffra and me. The piece was good and included the story on Valderrama, but it was still lacking the impact I hoped it would have. I called Brean and discussed the segments. She felt the same way but was happy that there was now some form of public exposure for the corruption on the part of lottery management. We hoped there would be some sort of inquiry from the governor or the education subcommittee based on the stories.

For the record, I am not disappointed in the work done by Goldstein. There is only so much you can cover in a ten-minute time slot and there was a lot of information involved. His segments got the stories out onto the Internet, where they will live forever. For several weeks, the segments were the first thing that popped up when you did an Internet search for California's lottery, which I felt was a win.

I copied and pasted both stories and sent them to the emails of several state senators and members of Congress. I also sent a link to Sheriff Ahern, who was one of the lottery commissioners. I didn't receive a response from anyone despite saying I had additional information and was willing to testify.

We drove back from Vegas on a Monday. I knew some sort of action would be coming in the next few days. Jeffra and I had covered our tracks fairly well throughout the process. I'd ensured that any version of the complaint to the state auditor wasn't on my computer, and I'd sent the redacted copies of all of the reports to the state auditor but kept a copy of the actual complaint for myself should I need it while being interviewed. At this point, we had placed all of our eggs in one basket by sending the complaint to the state auditor. We hoped to see some sort of action on their part because the walls would soon be closing in. It was nice to come back from a vacation in my favorite city as I prepared for what was coming. In retrospect. I probably should have taken a few more days.

CHAPTER 26

Go Home

Jeffra and I returned to work after the stories aired. We were in constant contact if we weren't in the office together. That week, Ortiz came by the office to collect our monthly paperwork, which was a little nerve-racking. I took a selfie from my desk with Ortiz in the background and sent it to Natalie with a text that said, "Uh oh." Ortiz didn't discuss the segment or anything other than the monthly paperwork. He left once he was done reviewing everything.

Unbeknownst to us, the CHP had opened an investigation into who appeared in the news story. There were whispers and rumors, but they eventually realized who it was. Dixon and Davis had already started pulling information from our state laptops. They pulled card access logs, phone records, emails, texts, and audits of the cases we had accessed in the SLED report writing system. Our every move was being tracked and researched.

We were smart enough to keep our whistleblower activities on our personal cell phones, which they wouldn't have access to without a search warrant. This wasn't something we were worried about because anything they did was going to be administrative. We had mostly accessed reports we had written ourselves, which we were permitted to do. Printing the reports wasn't a policy violation. All of our activities were allegedly protected because we had acted in good faith as whistleblowers reporting fraud, waste, and abuse. I assured myself we were bulletproof but still had stomachaches and anxiety every time I drove to the office.

One thing that still puzzles me is why the lottery assigned an internal investigation to Dixon, who was employed by the CHP. Kamala Harris' office wasn't being called in to conduct the investigation, which had been the recent practice. At this point, they had conducted three personnel investigations I was aware of. Dixon was directly involved in one of the claims Goldstein had reported on because he was the one who had approved the payment. Instead of Dixon being excluded because of potential conflict, he was given the opportunity to lead an investigation into Jeffra and me. The entire investigation could be called into question because of his bias toward the situation.

I started packing up my personal belongings from the office because I believed it was only a matter of time before I would be suspended or fired. It was surreal to think there was a possibility we would be removed, but I knew what had happened to Brean and Tacchini. As we discussed earlier, I am a nerd and my office was a reflection of that. I had Ghostbuster figures, football helmets, comic book statues, cop cars, challenge coins, movie posters, and various things that made me happy. I had worked for the lottery for over three years. I had accumulated plenty of things, which I had purchased for the office to make things better for Jim and me. Little things like a coffee maker, water pitcher, and other little trinkets. Everything fit into seven boxes. It was time to hope for the best and prepare for the worst.

Jeffra and I received an email from Ortiz on November 10, 2016. In the email, Ortiz said that he and Dixon wanted to meet with Jeffra and me on the morning of November 14. I knew they were planning on suspending us because Ortiz never showed up at our office in the morning. In the past, he would say he was going to arrive at ten and would show up at noon. It was time to face the consequences of our efforts, but I still assured myself we were fine.

I was so stressed Sunday night that I couldn't sleep. In a few hours, I would have to wake up to make sure I was on time for this meeting. There were several thoughts racing through my head about what to expect and what was going to happen to us. I finally fell asleep a few hours before my alarm went off. I got up and started my routine, which had been the same one for over three years. Make my first cup of coffee. Have breakfast while watching the news. Shave, take a shower, and pick out my clothes. I put on my belt, sliding it through each loop. I put on my handcuff case, my gun holster, and finally my badge.

I was issued badge #137 when I was hired by the lottery. The number thirteen was one of my lucky numbers, so having it on the badge made me happy. The badge had been with me through some tough times. I wore it to Aaron's funeral. It was on my belt when I was driving back to Sacramento several times in 2014 when my grandma was dying. I had cried while wearing that badge, I had bled while wearing that badge, and I was proud every time I put that badge to my belt. In a way, the badge was a friend who had my back through every good and bad day I had since the first time I put it on. I looked down at it one last time before I covered it with my overshirt. I realized this may be the last time I'd get to wear it.

I called Jeffra on my way to the office and discussed a game plan. I was starting to unravel a little because of the stress from the last several months and a complete lack of sleep. Jeffra was reassuring and reminded me we had done the right thing. He said there was nothing they could do to take that away from us. I told him it had been my pleasure to work with him and wished him luck as I pulled into the parking lot thirty minutes early. I saw Ortiz's car parked in front of the office and told Jeffra it looked like this would be an interesting morning. After we ended our call, I walked into Denny's to grab a cup of coffee because I figured they would be sitting in my office waiting for me. As I walked in, I was surprised to see a table full of suits sitting with Ortiz. I quickly turned around, walked out, and walked over to my office.

Once inside, I went into my office and closed the door. I sat at my desk for a few minutes and heard the beep of someone using their access card to open my office door. Dixon, Goulding, and Ortiz walked in. Goulding closed the door and placed his back against it, which clearly told me I was not free to leave. My heart started racing because, at that moment, I realized there were three of them and one of me. I had seen my fair share of movies and television shows where the snitch gets killed. Although this may have been a crazy place for my mind to wander, I was terrified.

Dixon informed me I was being suspended with pay and handed me a notice. He told me once I finished reading the notice, I would need to surrender everything I had been issued by the state to Ortiz. The notice stated that I was under investigation for allegations of misconduct for misuse of lottery information technology systems and violations of the lottery's "incompatible and inconsistent" activities statement. I would be required to remain at my residence during normal business hours and was only permitted to leave if I was instructed to by the lottery, or was on my lunch break. The notice also stated I would be interrogated by Dixon and Davis in forty-eight hours at the CHP station in Woodland Hills.

Dixon instructed me to surrender my firearm. I was concerned for my safety. We were in an office with no cameras and a closed door, which Goulding was blocking. By now, his firearm was visible, and I realized anything could happen to me in this critical moment. I slowly lifted up my shirt. I announced in a loud voice I was removing my firearm. First, I removed the magazine, and slowly removed my firearm from the holster. I placed the firearm and my badge on the desk. I surrendered my police credentials and access card. I informed them everything else was already in the office and asked Dixon if I should take my personal belongings with me. Dixon said I should and told me the interrogation was a formality. I wouldn't be coming back. At this point, I became defiant and angry but still maintained my composure as I told him I would need a ride home because I was surrendering my state car. Dixon said Ortiz would drive me home, so I could load my belongings into his trunk.

I marched in and out of the office with each of my boxes. Ortiz had to escort me each time during several trips. I was paraded in front of the lottery staff like many of the criminals I had walked out of the office in handcuffs. Even if I was returned to my position, the image would damage my reputation. Their decision to handle my suspension in this manner was meant to send a message. Dixon was growing visibly impatient by the time I was on box number 5. He told me I could come back after business hours if I wanted to collect the rest of my belongings. I thanked him for his offer but said I was almost done. After box number seven, I told Dixon I had forgotten about the foot locker I had purchased which was in the trunk of the state car. He was visibly agitated, which made me happy. It was my way of having some level of control over the situation.

Jim arrived at the office in the middle of Dixon serving me with my papers. He was intercepted by Davis, who took him to another office. Davis closed the door once they were inside and gave Jim the impression he wasn't allowed to leave. Unfortunately, Jim had to wait a while because I was in the middle of taking all of my boxes out one at a time. I was in Ortiz's car on the way home when he was pulled into our office and served me with his papers. Jim was walked through the same routine, but it took less time because he had nothing in our office. The lottery was a second career for Jeffra, so he left the decorating to me. The only thing he had to grab was his instant coffee container.

The ride home with Ortiz was awkward. I was upset, angry, and a little relieved all at the same time. I had lost what little respect I had for Ortiz over the last year, so spending this much time in a car with him felt like a cruel form of torture. We arrived at my place and I started unloading everything while he watched me. After I was done, I told him to have a good day and walked inside.

I had unloaded everything in my living room and stacked the boxes. I sat down and started at them, realizing what was happening. I had given over three years and countless hours of my life to the state of

California. During that time, I closed countless cases, received numerous restitution checks, commendations, and the most convictions in the state. My entire career had come down to this moment, and as much as I had prepared myself, the reality of it sent me into a deep depression. I felt broken, angry, hurt, and frustrated all at the same time. After making my calls to my union attorney, the exhaustion finally hit me. I lay down and fell asleep. When I woke up, it was dark outside. It was now after five, so I was allowed to leave my house in accordance with my orders from Dixon. Natalie and I went out to dinner. I called Brean and Tacchini and started preparing myself for the interrogation. The real fight was about to begin.

CHAPTER 27

Round One

I had never been in trouble as a peace officer, nor had I been the subject of an investigation. I always did my best to be courteous to everyone I encountered. I would take the time to discuss what led to someone being in handcuffs after I arrested them. I took the responsibility of being a peace officer seriously and remembered all of my past encounters with law enforcement, especially growing up in a poor community. I had positive and negative interactions with law enforcement. I wanted to be a part of changing the system by being the type of officer I would have wanted to interact with growing up. This belief guided me in everything I did and my actions that had led to my suspension and investigation.

My experience with interrogations had come from the ones I had conducted and the ones I had seen in cop shows. I knew what I was accused of, but I also knew what I had done was protected. This felt like a waste of my time. The union scheduled a conference call with me the day before my interrogation to go over what to expect and my actions that had led to the investigation. I had kept extensive mental notes and had already started keeping a journal of what the lottery had done. My summary of everything was sent to the union attorney the previous day. I was told the first thing Dixon and Davis would do is order me to answer all of their questions. I would face disciplinary action if I failed to answer. This was the easy way for an agency to fire personnel if their investigation was weak, which was the case here, so I had to be careful.

My union attorney asked me the important questions regarding engaging in misconduct. I went over everything Jeffra and I had done. We had attempted to address multiple issues internally before going to the auditor. I stood by our actions.

The union would later meet to discuss our actions to decide if they were within the scope of our employment before agreeing to represent us. If they decided our actions were outside of the scope of our employment, the union could drop us as a client. Hearing this bothered me, considering I had been a member of three different peace officer unions for several years. The unions seemed to have no problem representing individuals who were a disgrace to their badge and their oath. On-duty and off-duty cops who had committed crimes, driven drunk, and engaged in other horrendous acts. Unions proudly advertised when they won a case and got an officer reinstated for a variety of things that should have resulted in the officer losing their job. My union was questioning whistleblowing activities.

In response to the union's meeting, I recited the poster from the state auditor's office, which outlined my duty to report. I brought up the oath I took as a peace officer. I told the attorneys that my actions were in the best interest of the people of California and California's public schools. My actions were based on observing a pattern of behavior from the lottery. This behavior involved illegally paying out money that should have gone to public schools or the rightful owner of winning tickets. Taking funds away from public education. The idea of my union declining representation made a bad situation even worse. I was a little forceful when I defended my actions to the attorneys, especially when the lead union attorney had previously encouraged me to transfer to another department instead of supporting my whistleblower activities. Thankfully, the two attorneys who were assigned to the case were competent and supportive. The topic of not representing me wasn't discussed again.

On November 16, 2016, I pulled into the CHP parking lot. Dixon came across as being cocky and seemed to enjoy intimidating others. Past interrogations of lottery personnel had been conducted at lottery offices. He appeared to be sending me a message by scheduling my interrogation at a CHP office. Dixon was letting me know he was in control and I was on his turf. I arrived early and was greeted by my union attorney in the parking lot. We exchanged pleasantries and began discussing what to expect.

He gave me a last bit of advice and told me his role would be limited because he was mostly there to be a witness on my behalf. He hated the way CHP did their interrogations because it was always done the same way, which is death by paper. The interrogator will sit down with a huge stack of papers and hand exhibits to the subject of the interrogation one at a time. Each document will have to be reviewed. All of it is an intimidation tactic. The lawyer was a little salty, so I enjoyed him.

We entered the lobby and checked in with the desk officer. In my opinion, the CHP watch officer position was a joke, and based on my experience, it was a place where certified peace officers wasted taxpayer money. The watch officer sits at a computer and completes tasks that could have been done by employees who made a fraction of the pay. I was also a little jaded because of my experience working in the South Sacramento area office after being injured in the CHP academy.

Watch officer Mike Garcia and "bus officer" Joseph Pickar were hanging out in the front office on August 18th, 2009. Mark Anthony Wilson entered the lobby and approached the window. I was standing up front processing an accident report when I heard Wilson tell Pickar he was there to turn himself in. Wilson indicated he had a warrant and was tired of running. Pickar proceeded to tell Wilson he needed to go to the Sacramento Police Department if he wanted to turn himself in and handed him a piece of paper with their address. Wilson told Pickar the detectives he spoke to told him to turn himself into the state police, which Pickar shrugged off. Luckily, Garcia chimed in and told Pickar he should see what the warrant was for to make sure they weren't sending away "America's Most Wanted." Turns out, Wilson had actually been featured on *America's Most Wanted* and was wanted for murder. Trying to send a murder away didn't stop Pickar from being interviewed by the news for his big bust. I will never forget how big of a disgrace Pickar was, and my memory of the incident came rushing back to me as I stood there checking in. (Text, 2011)

Dixon escorted my lawyer and me to a conference room with a large table. I was admonished and told the interrogation would be recorded. We were seated across from Dixon and Davis. Dixon told me I was there as part of an internal investigation and was being directed to answer all questions. Dixon asked me to describe my assignment. I said I was a lottery investigator and was responsible for ensuring the honesty, integrity, and fairness of the operation of the lottery. I felt it was important to state my responsibilities early so it was on the record. This also made me feel better considering I was being interrogated for doing what I had been hired to do in the first place.

Dixon started handing me multiple documents, including my job description, the Law Enforcement Code of Ethics, and various memos I had signed when I started with the lottery. Among them was the Law Enforcement Code of Ethics, which is an ethos that peace officers subscribe to after being sworn in. Unfortunately, the contents were presented as "do as I say, not as I do" by Dixon, as he only focused on the portion concerning "whatever I see or hear of a confidential nature . . . in my official capacity will be kept ever secret, unless revelation is necessary for the performance of my duty." Dixon highlighted the section and ordered me to read it out loud. He only had me read one section while skipping over everything related to protecting the innocent from deception *and respecting the constitutional rights of all to liberty, equality, and justice.*

Dixon asked me what the portion of the oath meant to me. I said I would maintain confidential information unless it was necessary to reveal it in the performance of my duty of ensuring the honesty, integrity, and fairness of the California Lottery. This made me think of the many instances where the lottery had failed rightful owners of winning tickets by letting retailers claim tickets that were not lawfully theirs, and receive payments. I thought about Hung Nguyen who was denied over one million dollars because he lost his Powerball ticket and didn't have the money to hire a lawyer. I thought about Noam Kashanian, who lottery officials changed the rules for to give him the ability to claim a prize under the same circumstances because he could hire a lawyer. I thought about the money paid to individuals who had committed fraud. I thought about the unsuspecting victims who were told they couldn't claim a prize because they weren't a citizen. It was apparent the picture Dixon was painting didn't address the issues; it was portraying me as the bad guy who shared confidential information and the lottery was the victim.

Over the next hour, Dixon continued to hand me one document at a time. It looked like he was building his case against me for sharing confidential information with the media. Dixon's approach was laughable because he thought I would be caught in a lie for accessing reports I had written. I admitted to accessing each of my reports. Dixon covered individual user credentials, accessing the report writing system, and various other mundane materials. I couldn't help but have a bit of joy because I couldn't wait to tell him how wrong he was because he was actively interrogating me for engaging in protected whistleblower activities. His arrogance and apparent ignorance gave me a false sense of security.

Dixon handed me a document that contained the text for section 502 of the California Penal Code. This section covered illegal access of a government computer. I was under the impression I was the subject of an administrative investigation related to violating lottery policies and not a criminal violation. I had charged multiple suspects with this section during felony investigations. I asked Dixon if I was being investigated for committing a crime? Dixon said they were exploring all violations, including criminal conduct. I was now aware I would be fighting to keep my job, my reputation, and potentially my freedom.

Knowing I was being accused of committing a felony by accessing cases I wrote and information I was authorized to review created a new level of stress. There was a sudden weight in my chest. I felt the fight or flight I only experienced while responding to an emergency or fighting with individuals I was arresting. Dixon reiterated that all of my statements during the interrogation were compelled and couldn't be used against me in criminal proceedings. I still couldn't help but feel like I was being set up. I wouldn't lose my freedom, but if given the chance Dixon would take away my reputation.

Dixon continued lobbing policies at me until we got to one which piqued my interest. I was given an email sent to me by Human Resources titled "Whistleblower notification." The state of California annually reminded all state employees of their duty to report fraud, waste, or abuse on the part of their employer. The ironic thing about Dixon having me review this particular document, and reading it out loud for the record, is it specifically stated I was supposed to report fraud, waste, or abuse to the state auditor. It was particularly ironic to say out loud that whistleblowers can expect to be free from retaliation for doing so. After reading the pertinent information back to Dixon, on the record, he asked me if there was anything in the document which instructed me to provide reports to anyone other than the state auditor. I said there was nothing in the document which stated I was prohibited from doing so. Dixon apparently thought he'd catch me on a technicality by saying I took my concerns about fraud, waste, and abuse to the media instead of through proper internal channels.

Dixon continued to press me on the document. He asked me if there was anything in the document which authorized me to provide the California state auditor, as an employee, of the lottery, confidential or sensitive documents. This question was meant to be a "gotcha" because Dixon intended to show I wasn't authorized to provide the reports and other documents Jim and I had sent the auditor's office. The line of questioning was odd because it seemed like Dixon already knew we had been in contact with the state auditor's office. I simply recited the section of the document which asked to support what you allege by providing evidence and copies of documents. I felt like I was in control of the interrogation because I was able to squash each argument Dixon was trying to establish. I was using the documents he was *introducing as evidence against him.*

Dixon continued presenting me with documents. We reviewed document after document about dates and times I accessed my office. He would press me on accessing files that showed investigations into questionable claims. The majority of the files involved investigations that produced evidence showing the tickets being claimed by retailers were actually taken from their rightful owners. Dixon pressed me on the Valderrama claim and what right I had to access it. Dixon was painting a picture of me as a rogue investigator. I was insubordinate because I didn't notify my superiors of the investigation Jim and I had conducted into the conduct of lottery management.

Dixon's line of questioning led us to the documents and database copies I had provided to the state auditor. The documents provided the auditor with specific cases for review, which showed exactly how the lottery was misappropriating public funds. Dixon asked me directly who I provided copies of the documents to. I called for a short break for a dramatic pause. After the short break, I returned to the interrogation room. I told Dixon about the report Jim and I made to the auditor, who we sent the documents to as evidence. Dixon went back and forth with me on policies and the semantics of how doing the right thing isn't always doing the right thing. Dixon then asked why I copied the contents of the Valderrama into a word document as opposed to printing out the entire report. I informed Dixon I had done so because the audit for the report showed he and Libby had printed out a copy. Payment was authorized for Valderrama despite the evidence showing he was not the lawful owner of the ticket he claimed. I told Dixon I knew I would be providing the auditor with a copy of the report.

After an eternity of semantics on document formatting and permitted use for the reports I had written, it was time to discuss my appearance on the Goldstein report. Dixon asked a line of silly questions relating to how I got to the news studio and what routes I took. He then asked me who was with me. I mentioned Jim and

Natalie. Dixon asked me for Natalie's contact information. I asked if was required to give it to him. Dixon stated I was because she was a witness to his internal investigation, but I could ask her if she wished to speak with him. I provided him with her information as ordered. None of this sat well with me because I didn't trust Dixon or the CHP. I worked in law enforcement for several years. I had seen and heard of harassment and intimidation by law enforcement. Sitting in a CHP office instead of a lottery office only reinforced my concerns. Natalie told my lawyer she wasn't required to participate in an administrative investigation and told my attorney to tell Dixon the same. He did.

The interrogation pressed on for what felt like an eternity. We covered my appearance on the investigative report, the hopes Jim and I had that the report would create public outrage and presentation of documents. Dixon circled back to the Kashanian report and old emails about not accessing it without approval from Tacchini, who was no longer there. Dixon was visibly upset when I pushed back at every "truth" he threw at me when following directives from previous management. Dixon and Libby had frequently told the staff that old directives from previous management were not to be followed, so I was using their past statements against him.

Although I felt confident in my situation, I had no idea I was about to be caught completely off guard. Dixon presented me with a document and asked me to describe it to him for the record. It was the first page of the written complaint I had mailed to the state auditor. At that moment, I knew everything Jim and I did had no impact. The complaint found its way back to the lottery, which I believe to this day was intentional. It now made sense. Despite several phone calls and a packet of evidence, nobody from the auditor's office called us. Tacchini reported his concerns to Kamala Harris and was relieved of his position. No matter what I said, or what evidence I had to support doing the right thing, my law enforcement career was over. Dixon claimed he "found" the document in my office, on the desk of a former investigator. This would mean I was careless and simply left evidence of being a whistleblower sitting on a desk.

As we neared the conclusion of my interrogation, Dixon gave me the opportunity to close out by making a statement. This was my opportunity to justify my actions and provide my side of the story. This was a textbook tactic I had used during countless interviews and interrogations. I viewed it as an opportunity to present the internal failures by lottery management to address issues Jim, myself, and several other current and former investigators had brought to their attention. Issues that fell on deaf ears, or were explained away as being best for business. After all, as Libby said, we were loss prevention with peace officer powers.

After a short break, I returned with a sense of purpose. I opened by bringing up the fact I had wanted the investigator job since 2010 when I unsuccessfully interviewed for an open position. I believed in what the lottery did by providing funding to schools, and protecting that money was something I believed in. I mentioned conducting myself in an ethical and professional manner and being honest about the issues I had observed with lottery management. After trying unsuccessfully to have multiple issues addressed with no action, I put my career on the line by contacting the auditor's office. My hope was bringing in an outside entity to address lottery management putting educational money in the hands of the underserving, and in some cases, criminals would result in positive change.

I attempted to continue with my closing statement but was overcome with sadness and grief. I knew the deck was stacked against me. Despite doing what was right, the correct way, this was how my law enforcement career would end. I was broken. I began sobbing in my chair in a way that I had not sobbed since my grandfather died when I was a kid. I cried, attempted to speak through the sobs. A part of me died in that moment. The part of me that believed in the system working, in the good guys being protected, in really anything being just, died in that moment.

Dixon continued the interrogation by reviewing my statements. I was able to somewhat mutter my concerns about the lottery's continued failures to address multiple issues in between sobbing. Everything I said from that moment on came from a place of defeat. Dixon reminded me we were not there to discuss the issues with the lottery or their failures to address concerns. I felt it was relevant after three years of bringing issues to lottery management's attention, but I just wanted it to end. Finally, after four and a half hours, it did. (Dixon, Transcrption of Audio Recording-Galbreath, 2016)

CHAPTER 28

The Aftermath

I walked out of the CHP office and spoke briefly with my attorney. I started my drive home and called Natalie to tell her about what had happened. We talked for a bit, and I finally arrived home. I sat down on the corner of my bed started crying again. In that moment, I didn't want to live and would have taken the opportunity to be dead. I had many bad thoughts while sitting there alone. I felt defeated. I felt like my life had been sent into a tailspin. I felt like doing what I thought was the right thing, the thing I had sworn to do when I became a cop, was complete bullshit. There was anger at my law enforcement academy for training me to always do the right thing—always speak up. They didn't provide training on what to do when you don't want to live because you spoke up, and are being punished.

Most of all, I was angry at myself. I should have listened when the head union attorney told me not to speak up, to ignore the issues, and just find another department. As much as I thought he was a spineless tool at the time, I now realized he was right. He knew what would happen to Jim and me by going down this path, which was the reason he refused to help us. The doubt and depression far outweighed the sense of purpose I previously felt. This feeling would only get worse in the coming weeks.

The next day, Jeffra went to the CHP office for his interrogation. Dixon's approach with Jeffra was slightly different than mine. Dixon went over Jeffra's law enforcement career prior to handing him the duty statement for lottery investigators. Jeffra read the duty statement with a sense of defiance, even saying "gotcha" in his own way when he was done. Dixon focused on the Law Enforcement Code of Ethics with Jeffra. Dixon brought up confidential information and keeping your private life unsullied. It seemed like Dixon's approach was to attack Jeffra's age, experience, and integrity to show he knew better and shouldn't have been a whistleblower. Although the tone of the interrogation was slightly different, Dixon followed the same formula. He presented Jeffra with multiple documents, slowly building toward his intent of showing he knew better. Dixon wanted to show Jeffra had violated policy by engaging in whistleblower activity.

When Dixon got to the information security portion of his document review, he made a very telling statement. Dixon said he knew Jeffra had worked in a "traditional" law enforcement agency prior to working for the lottery. Dixon said that the lottery had a law enforcement branch but it was really a "corporate entity," which reinforced what Jeffra and I believed all along. The lottery was being operated by individuals who didn't view their positions as being part of a publicly funded agency. Lottery management treated their positions as if they were part of a private business. This meant trying to address issues internally was a complete waste of time. The lottery management team believed they didn't have to follow the same rules, laws, and regulations as other government agencies. The sad thing was having a "peace officer" from the CHP refusing to follow his oath of office and believing the conduct was acceptable. The belief was that anyone trying to address problems by reporting them to the outside agency expected to investigate state agency misconduct was the enemy.

Dixon pressed Jeffra on releasing documents to allied agencies and how internal policies failed to make such a release a "business" purpose. Jeffra reminded Dixon of the lottery regularly working with allied agencies, which Libby and Dixon actively encouraged us to do when referring all crimes to local law enforcement. Dixon continued with his ludicrous line of questioning and eventually received the business end of Jeffra's bluntness. Jeffra looked Dixon in the eyes and told him all of this was common sense.

Dixon moved on to the Valderrama case by asking Jeffra if he was familiar with it. Jeffra was brutally honest. He mentioned the contents of the case, specifically saying Valderrama had been caught lying. Jeffra mentioned the press release put out by the lottery. He described it as a "total fabrication." All Dixon could respond with was, "okay."

Dixon continued the interrogation by asking Jeffra why we chose to take our story to the news media. Jeffra brought up the lottery's history of firing or removing individuals who spoke up regarding their concerns. It was hard for Dixon to argue there wasn't a pattern based on what had happened to Brean and Tacchini, especially when you factored in our current situation. Dixon said our activity was protected, so he didn't understand why we would be fearful. Dixon then pivoted his questions. He called into question our legal right to access the databases which contained our investigative reports for the purpose of providing evidence to the state auditor. Dixon insisted our access for the purpose of providing evidence of our allegations was unlawful and claimed the "data" we accessed belonged to the lottery. Jeffra responded by bringing up the countless embezzlement cases he had investigated, which the lottery could have prevented. Jeffra mentioned bringing the issues he had observed to the attention of appropriate internal units and lottery management. He saw no action because he kept having cases assigned to him involving the same issue he had tried to correct.

Jeffra brought up the way Libby had treated us during our first meeting. Libby said the lottery could be run like a corporation. Jeffra mentioned his phone call with Dixon where he specifically mentioned the embezzlement issues and lack of fiduciary responsibility from the lottery. Lastly, he mentioned the complete lack of action on the part of Libby, Dixon, and the lottery to address any of the issues brought to their attention. Dixon asked Jeffra if he would agree the lottery was a corporation. Jeffra told Dixon it wasn't a corporation. The lottery was a state agency. He told Dixon there were no articles of incorporation for the lottery, and he had investigated plenty of corporations, so he would know. Dixon corrected himself by saying there was "some business aspect to what we do."

Dixon attempted to recover his fumbled line of questioning. He moved on to his assertion about the correct individuals being paid in the cases we submitted to the state auditor. Dixon asked Jeffra if he had "all of the facts and information" contained by upper management when they had decided to pay Mr. Kashanian. Dixon said he would concede that Jim was entitled to his opinion, but his opinion wasn't "based on all of the facts" when the decision was made by executive management to pay or not pay a claim. Dixon failed to mention the requirement that those decisions needed to be based on regulatory compliance because this was public money meant for schools, not discretionary funds from a private corporation.

Dixon put his ignorance of lottery statutes on full display when he asserted you can be defined as the "winner" of a ticket when you direct someone else to purchase and scratch-off the play area of a ticket. Jeffra corrected Dixon and told him the definition of the winner of a scratch-off ticket is pretty specific. Dixon stuttered as he told Jim he was correct. Dixon showed his true colors and started getting unprofessional and condescending. Jeffra's union attorney would have to redirect Dixon several times to keep him on task. He went on to justify the actions in the Valderrama case, admitting he was the author of the supplemental portion of the report that made the decision to pay Valderrama. This was done despite the evidence showing he wasn't the rightful owner of the ticket. Jeffra's interrogation ended shortly after Dixon once again brought up the Law Enforcement Code of Ethics and appearing on an investigative report, attempting again to catch him in a lie.

During the interrogation, and unbeknownst to me, it was revealed Jeffra had made the decision to retire. Jeffra would call me after his retirement was official to tell me about it and his decision to not see this through to the end while staying employed with the state. The union had discussed termination with Jeffra, and him possibly being ineligible to receive retirement. Jeffra returned to public service after retiring from the sheriff's department, and had worked hard to earn the additional retirement. Not trusting the lottery to do the right thing and not wanting to leave his family hanging, he made the decision to retire after giving his final statement during his interrogation. While I completely understood his reasoning, I felt alone. (Dizon, Transcript of Audio Recording-Jeffra, 2016)

CHAPTER 29

Let The Games Begin

I felt like a criminal for the first time in my life. Being on paid administrative time off felt like house arrest. I didn't leave my apartment, which was nice in a way because I started catching up on shows I hadn't had the time to watch and playing video games I hadn't had the time to play. When I looked out my window, I would occasionally see unmarked state vehicles rolling down my street, ensuring I hadn't left my residence. The lottery was wasting public money yet again, but I was beginning to accept my fate. I had followed all protocols up until this point and knew I would be okay if the lottery was stupid enough to fire me, so I wouldn't risk it on a technicality by going somewhere during the day.

I would hang out with Natalie and some of my friends in the evenings once I was off house arrest. It was nice to leave my place because it felt like a prison, which is funny considering almost everyone would be working from home a few years later. Dixon didn't take Natalie's refusal to speak with him well. He was calling Natalie several times a day. She wouldn't answer his calls or answer calls from a blocked number. He was getting agitated because he stopped leaving messages and would just hang up once the call went to voicemail. Dixon called me one evening around 7 p.m. I let the call go to voicemail because he could have called me at any point during the day when I was at home. Dixon left me a voicemail informing me he would be searching my desk and just wanted me to know. It was just another intimidation tactic, so I ignored it because there was nothing for him to find. Jim had retired, so I just assumed he was bored and needed someone to harass.

In early December, I received a call from Ortiz. He told me we needed to meet in person so he could serve me with a new interrogation letter. He gave me a letter informing me I was scheduled for a second interrogation with Dixon. This time around, I would have Danielle Hash as my attorney, who had been a great ally for me throughout the process. Prior to the interrogation, I met Hash. We discussed the first interrogation, Dixon's conduct, and his obsession with speaking with Natalie. We agreed Dixon would probably try to have me call Natalie from my phone, so she knew to not answer my call.

We arrived at the CHP office and were seated in the same conference room. Dixon said there was some business we needed to address before we get started. He said Natalie had refused to take his calls. Danielle reminded Dixon he was told by my previous attorney she would not talk to him. Dixon said he wanted to hear that from her and ordered me to call her on speakerphone from my cell. After the call went to voicemail, Dixon told us he was going to talk to her one way or another. Dixon then threatened Natalie and told us, to tell her, that he would sit outside of her home if he had to. Dixon was fixated and was now resorting to threats because he had nothing else at his disposal.

The phone call and his threat set the tone for what would be a much shorter but more aggressive interrogation. Dixon recapped the previous interrogation and cut me off each time I attempted a rebuttal to his statements. Dixon brought up the perjury case he previously said wouldn't be criminally prosecuted. I reminded him of his desire to not pursue criminal charges and the fact Ortiz had talked me through changing the entire report. It was important to get this situation on the record because it was the situation that resulted in my decision to be a whistleblower. Dixon briefly argued the semantics of opening a criminal investigation into the retailer. He quickly changed the subject to the reports I had printed out as evidence.

Dixon pressed me on providing "an entity outside of the state lottery with information you obtained from our information technology infrastructure." It was Dixon's way of "proving" I violated policy when I printed out the reports as evidence for our whistleblower complaint. Dixon knew those actions were protected but continued to focus on our supplying documents to the auditor. He continued to mention supplying reports to an entity outside of the state lottery" during the rest of the interrogation.

Dixon instructed me to place the reports I gave to the state auditor, or as he again put it, "an entity outside of the state lottery" on the table. His demeanor was hostile, so Hash asked if we could take a moment to unpack his request. Dixon appeared agitated and snapped at Hash, who reminded him she wasn't being interrogated. Dixon was consistently demeaning to Hash, but she held her own every time. Dixon's continued his line of questioning, saying I had provided confidential information to an entity outside of the state lottery, even stopping himself at one point when he started to say state auditor. I ultimately had the last laugh when reading the final report, which referenced Dixon talking to the state auditor's office. He was told by a representative from the office that they were permitted to receive all of the documents I had sent them.

The interrogation ended a little over two hours after it began with Dixon taking a few jabs at my integrity before we concluded. Hash and I parted ways, and this time around, I didn't feel as sad because I knew everything was on the table.

A little over a week had passed since my interrogation, and my paid time off was set to expire the next day. The day went on with no word from the lottery on my employment status. After my mail was delivered with nothing from the lottery, I decided to reach out to Dottie Wallace, who was the director of Human Resources. I sent her an email a little after 4:30 p.m. and said I hadn't heard anything, so I was assuming someone would be at the office the next day to let me in. I received an email from Wallace at 5:36 p.m. informing me that my paid time off was being extended another thirty days. Wallace followed up with a voicemail saying they had "forgotten" to send the notice. This would happen two more times before all was said and done. Each time it was almost an hour after normal business hours and was followed up by a frantic call from Wallace. In addition to the late notice, I didn't receive pay stubs and even had my W2 sent to the wrong address. The state of California imposed heavy fines on private employers who engaged in similar conduct based on employee complaints. The state had a law that exempted them from the same penalties. In addition to knowingly grossly misappropriating public funds, I realized lottery management was also incompetent.

I had a discussion with Natalie about the interrogation and Dixon's threat. Although we both came from law enforcement and generally trusted those in the profession, we also had first-hand knowledge of how an unhinged member of law enforcement can impact someone's life. In this case, our primary concern was Dixon showing up outside and confronting her in a manner that made her feel threatened. It wasn't far-fetched to believe he would do something to put her in a position where she felt cornered. While law enforcement can be a noble profession that attracts the best in our communities, it can also attract the unethical who abuse their power. There are plenty of law enforcement members who are dangerous and know how to manipulate the system. One thing I had always loved about being an investigator was being mostly on my own and my professional circle being small. It was filled with people I trusted.

Our minds were focused on possible outcomes. Dixon continuing to call Natalie several times a day and hanging up didn't help matters. In December of 2016, Natalie made the decision to call CHP Internal Affairs to report Dixon's harassment and threat. Natalie provided the investigator with specifics regarding the threat and the frequency of his calls. Natalie informed the investigator of the law enforcement background of her and her family, which showed she knew the laws and procedures Dixon should have been following. Dixon abruptly retired. He received his state pension. The investigator never called back to discuss their findings.

I also made the decision to contact CHP Internal Affairs to report Libby's failure to abide by his peace officer oath and allow public funds to be diverted. I had a lengthy discussion with an investigator regarding everything I had experienced, including Libby cursing at me during our first meeting. A short time later, Libby was "reassigned" from his position with the lottery and returned to the CHP, where was promoted to assistant chief. The investigator didn't call me back to discuss their findings. While my concerns were easily dismissed as being a bitter employee under investigation, the timing of his reassignment was interesting. (Dizon, Transcript of Audio Recording-Galbreath , 2016) (Unknown, Chronological Summary, 2016)

CHAPTER 30

The Fall Out

I was still sitting at home being paid to not leave my house during business hours when 2017 started. Every day, I would wake up and check the state auditor's website for a report on the lottery. I would listen to local talk radio hosts John and Ken, who frequently talked about government corruption hoping to hear something, but it never happened. Life started to feel like *Groundhog Day*.

On January 9th, 2017, I received word that LaBrie had been removed from the lottery. I was excited because it appeared we had accomplished something, but the excitement was short-lived. It turned out LaBrie was appointed to the California Gambling Control Commission by Governor Brown, which included a nice yearly salary of $142,095. This hardly seemed like a reprimand—more of a shuffling around of personnel. I had hoped it would be an indication of things to come, but ultimately the state auditor's report of their investigation into our complaint would never be released. (Simmons, 2017)

On March 28, 2017, four months after I had originally been suspended, I was called to my office, where I was served with termination paperwork by Goulding and Ortiz. Libby and Dixon were both gone, so the meeting was fairly informal. The lottery cited multiple violations that were said to justify my termination. The lottery said I had engaged in incompatible and inconsistent activity which was in conflict with my duties as a state employee. They said I had failed to safeguard claimant information by providing redacted reports to the state auditor. The nail in my coffin was the lottery saying I had committed a felony by accessing reports I had previously written, was dishonest, and released confidential information to the general public. The dishonesty allegation alone would prevent me from ever working in law enforcement again, which was something the lottery knew.

I called Hash, who reviewed the termination and informed me the lottery failed to follow basic peace officer personnel policy. They hadn't given me copies of their "evidence" when they served me with my termination notice. As a result of their incompetence, I was re-hired and placed on another paid suspension until April 18 when I was called back to the office and fired again. This time, they had their paperwork in order.

In addition to my union representation, I sought my own external legal counsel to represent me. The union would also not represent me in a civil case. I retained the counsel of Santiago & Jones. David Jones, Art Santiago, and Alex Vo took on my case and agreed to represent me. Jeffra ended up signing up with them as well since he was denied an honorable retirement by the lottery.

Prior to filing a lawsuit, I was required to go through a settlement conference with the California State Personnel Board, which occurred a few months later. I entered the hearing room with Hash and Jones. The attorney general's office, which was still being overseen by Harris, represented the lottery. After listening to the lottery representative and their Department of Justice attorney rattle off their list of charges, I was offered two months' salary and the ability to resign in lieu of termination. This essentially meant I was acknowledging I had engaged in wrongdoing. I was hurting financially, which was probably why they waited two months before scheduling the conference. Most people would probably be forced to take the scraps in order to survive, but at this point, my reputation was on the line. I declined their settlement offer and moved forward with a full "hearing," which would be scheduled several months later.

CHAPTER 31

See You in Court!

Following the conference, Alex, David, and I sat down for a meeting to discuss our next steps. I had kept notes on my complaint and investigation, and I had written responses to every notice I received from the lottery. As a result, there were several large binders full of evidence. I decided I was ready to move forward with filing a lawsuit, which meant my situation would no longer be private and would become public record. Deciding to file a lawsuit isn't as easy as you might think because it means you are sharing your story with anyone who decides to search court records.

The thing that kept running through my head was the report the lottery provided me regarding Dixon and Davis' "investigation." As previously discussed, Dixon had called the state auditor before he retired and sought information about the reporting process. He asked the representative what documents they were legally allowed to receive. The state auditor representative told Dixon they were legally authorized to receive confidential documents but then went on to say the state auditor doesn't endorse or request whistleblowers to proactively obtain evidence. This statement was in direct conflict with the notice state employees receive every year. The state auditor representative contradicted what they put out in writing, and Dixon "found" the first page of my whistleblower complaint on a desk. It just didn't make sense.

Although I still wanted to be a peace officer, I didn't want to go back to the lottery. I had no faith in the state system doing what was right. This was further supported after Hash presented evidence to the State Personnel Board to have me reinstated and have my termination dismissed. Hash cited the lottery's vague evidence and factual inaccuracies. The State Personnel Board's administrative law judge sided with the lottery. After several months of beating myself up and realizing the only way to truly clear my name was to fight, I was ready to move forward with a lawsuit.

Vo filed the lawsuit with Los Angeles County in August of 2017. I was excited and relieved at the same time. The state had scheduled my Personnel Board hearing for October. The hearing was a required formality, but it would allow both sides to call witnesses and would be the first official hearing that would allow testimony regarding what had occurred. I was looking forward to getting the chance for everyone to go on the record and had come up with more than thirty witnesses who would be called to testify.

A few weeks before the attorney general's office reached out to Jones and asked to go to mediation prior to the hearing. We agreed to mediation and met the Friday before my hearing was scheduled to start, which was waiting until the last possible moment. The mediation lasted most of the day and isn't something I can discuss, having signed a non-disclosure agreement.

What I can comment on is my official peace officer employment record because there's nothing barring me from discussing factual information. My official lottery employee records contain no mention of any investigation into misconduct or being terminated. They also contain my past evaluations, replete with high marks and commendations I received for my investigative work. The California Commission on Peace Officer Standards and Training shows my official peace officer employment status as a resignation from the state lottery. The official record contains no mention of what occurred or why. In a perfect world, I would be considered an exemplary peace officer and investigator because that's what the official record says. I suppose you can say I cleared my name and won. So now what? (Auditor, 2016)

CHAPTER 32

So, Now What?

It's been five years since Jeffra and I made the decision to become whistleblowers. Five years since Brean was fired for questioning why LaBrie would pay someone over a million dollars when the evidence showed they weren't entitled to it, taking away money that would have gone to California Public Schools. Five years since Tacchini asked Kamala Harris to investigate the state lottery for gross misconduct, which resulted in the governor removing him from office. Five years that the California state auditor's office has been in possession of a complaint that clearly shows misappropriation of public funds on the part of lottery management and retaliation at the highest levels involving the state attorney general. A lot can happen in five years.

The California Lottery continued to be plagued by stories of financial mismanagement and misconduct by its executive management. In five years, the lottery has had two deputy directors and the law enforcement division has been a revolving door of leadership from the CHP. Hugo Lopez "resigned" after a slew of stories made the media rounds regarding lavish spending on trinkets. An audit of lottery spending was released by the state controller's office, which revealed $300,000 in inappropriate spending. Photographs of lottery management acting inappropriately during travel funded with public money were leaked, which included a manager with his head up a women's shirt. In Lopez's resignation email, he bragged about the lottery revenue growing to $7 billion annually but made no mention of the multitude of scandals that plagued the lottery or how much of those sales involved prize money that was illegally paid out.

In February of 2020, California State Auditor Elaine Howle finally released the results of an audit which looked at the activity of lottery management from 2017 forward. The findings stated the lottery existed to "maximize funding for education, but the lottery has not prioritized this funding when setting its budgets and, thus, hasn't funded education at the required level." The report showed lottery management had consistently entered into non-competitive agreements with vendors. In the fiscal year of 2017–2018, the lottery should have provided public education with $36 million more than it actually paid. The audit also revealed the lottery didn't have up-to-date analysis of the optimal balance between prize payouts and education funding, so it didn't know if too much money was being diverted to prize payments. The lottery's most current analysis was over ten years old.

The audit called the current "oversight from the state controller's office ineffective. The audit revealed that the SCO had actually removed a portion of their 2019 audit report, which called into question the lottery spending over $720,000 related to agreements with hotels for trade shows. The lottery couldn't provide any proof that it had even explored other options before entering into agreements with the hotels.

The portion of the report containing this information was removed by the SCO at the request of the lottery. The SCO also allowed the lottery to write its "independent" audit, which was then presented to the state legislature. The report stated that the lottery wasn't following the regulations it was legally required to follow regarding how it budgeted money for public schools.

The procurement practices, which included selecting independent auditing firms and targeting Hispanic advertising, didn't follow regulations for entering into non-competitive agreements. This was the case in eight of the fifteen agreements the auditor reviewed. These agreements were worth $5.7 million. The report went on to recommend the state legislature require the lottery to pay back the $36 million to public schools. (Howle, 2020) (Unknown, Report 2019-112 Fact Sheet, 2020)

This report was released after intense scrutiny from the news media and elected officials who "demanded answers" after additional whistleblower stories were revealed, shedding light on misconduct from lottery management. The lottery released a statement where it "strongly disagreed" with owing, as the lottery stated, $69 million to public education, citing a "fundamental difference of opinion" over the interpretation of the Lottery Act. The lottery also bragged about the auditor not finding any issues with its investigative "approaches" for awarding prize claims. This was clearly a dig at everyone who had gone to the auditor to specifically cite the issues with the "investigative approach" not being followed. Lottery management chose to pay individuals who weren't entitled to receive funds per the lottery regulations they were supposed to adhere to.

The response from the lottery encouraged Howle to contact Roberto Zavala should she have any additional questions. For those keeping score, this is the same person I went to in my first year about internal flaws regarding prize payments—and who handpicked the "independent" auditor who looked at the lottery every year. Interestingly enough, in all the years the independent auditor was conducting their audits of the lottery, they never discovered the issues uncovered by the state auditor's office. Zavala has since retired. (Johnson, California State Lottery Response to Draft Audit Report 2019-112, 2020)

As a result of the audit report, California Republican Senator Ling Ling Chang introduced SB-891 which would have required the lottery to pay back the money it owed to public schools and would ensure funding for public schools stayed consistent, which the Lottery Act was apparently not doing. I reached out to Chang's office several times to provide a first-hand account of what I witnessed. She, like every elected official I reached out to, never called me back. The bill ultimately died, and I found no record of the lottery ever paying back the money it owed. (Chang, 2020)

The auditor's report didn't address the issues brought to their attention by Brean, Jeffra, or myself. I requested copies of the state auditor's investigation into my complaint through a Public Records Request Act (PRA). The auditor's legal representative sent me an email saying they didn't have to comply with a PRA because they needed to protect the identity of whistleblowers. I responded by giving my consent to reveal my identity—to myself. I was still denied. In the end, I was just disappointed that the auditor said nothing about our complaint and then took years to release a report involving new ones. The auditor chooses to not focus on multiple other issues that had occurred in years prior, which indicated that public schools were owed much more than they believed.

Kamala Harris went on to become a senator, and eventually vice president of the United States. Seeing the country swoon over her was hard to watch, especially when she made statements about the need to protect whistleblowers from Donald Trump. This was the same person who choose to take no action when a whistleblower asked her office to investigate lottery management, which resulted in him being removed from his appointment. The same person whose office "defended" the lottery when I sued them for whistleblower retaliation and investigated Brean for misconduct when she reported lottery management misappropriating public funds.

Jeffra is enjoying his retirement. He stays busy with private investigations, book writing, and his grandkids. The lottery spent the last five years fighting his lawsuit and trying to unsuccessfully get it dismissed. They finally settled last year after their final appeal was overturned by the court. They still failed to admit to any wrongdoing.

As for me? I'm still trying to figure that out. I have struggled with deciding what's next while trying to get my footing. I stopped trying to work in law enforcement after two separate agencies choose not to move forward with me after I passed their background investigations. They were nice enough to warn me after my conditional job offer that my status as a whistleblower would be a tough sell. Although the official record states that I did nothing wrong and was never fired, there will always be a stigma associated with being a whistleblower. I obtained my

California private investigator's license, worked in various security management positions, and left the state. I even dabbled in health insurance fraud, which is a story all its own. Luckily, I managed to meet two of my best friends in the process.

What's the moral of my story? There are various levels of right and wrong when dealing with government employment. There are some noble and corrupt people who work in government. Trying to identify the good guys is an exercise in insanity. The system doesn't support those who speak up or speak out when something is wrong. Stories continue to pile up about government corruption and the "rules for thee, but not for me" we see almost every day.

What I find the most disheartening is reading stories like what happened to Michael McQueary and Carmyn Fields. McQueary is the whistleblower who exposed the Jerry Sandusky crimes at Penn State after initially reporting them in 2001. He reported the crimes to university officials, who choose to do nothing. He was fired after cooperating with investigators and naming names. After being labeled as a whistleblower and fired, he found himself to be damaged goods. Fields worked for the CHP, where she was continuously sexually harassed by another member of the department. Fields complained to CHP management about the sexual harassment she received multiple times, but no action was taken. She was repeatedly denied promotions and said she was treated more like a suspect than a victim. She was required to resign from her position when she decided to settle her lawsuit against the CHP, which was a common requirement of the state when they settled lawsuits. State law was changed to prohibit the practice in 2021. The reality is that whistleblowers aren't protected when they speak up. They're only awarded a small amount of money for retaliation in most cases because the whistleblower is forced to settle in order to survive.

I don't have the secrets to winning the lottery. The only way to cheat is to manipulate the system, usually with the help of an attorney, and hope you receive the support of lottery management, who doesn't want bad press. If you really want to help public schools, just donate your money directly to the school or any program that helps the underserved in your community. Better yet, volunteer your time because that's the most valuable thing you can do for schools. I firmly believe the lotteries in all states should be evaluated to determine the actual benefit to public schools. If the lottery in a single-party state like California can lack appropriate oversight, then what are the odds it's occurring in other states?

In the end, I don't regret my decision to speak up, but my union attorney was unfortunately right when he told me I would be giving up my career and my retirement. As I watch continuing acts of injustice and corruption, I hope for a day when whistleblowers are truly protected.

The End

www.ingramcontent.com/pod-product-compliance
Lightning Source LLC
Chambersburg PA
CBHW052128270326
41930CB00012B/2802